REAL ESTATE TERMS POCKET DICTIONARY

A Quick Reference Guide to Over 500 of the
Most Important Real Estate Terms

BY

THE REAL ESTATE TRAINING TEAM

IMPORTANT DISCLAIMERS

The information contained within this book is strictly for informational purposes. The author and publisher do not make any guarantee as to the accuracy of this work. The author does not assume and hereby disclaims any liability to any party for any loss, damage, or disruption caused by errors or omissions, whether such errors or omissions result from accident, negligence, or any other cause. We are not responsible for your actions and cannot guarantee results or success. The use of the information in this book or any products and services recommended should be based on your own due diligence and you agree that our company is not liable for any success or failure in your business that is directly or indirectly related to the purchase and use of our information, products, or services.

TABLE OF CONTENTS

PREFACE

This book contains additional resources for the aspiring real estate professional. Since they could not be physically included in the book, they are all available to download on our website www.therealestate trainingteam.com. This includes helpful videos, free resources, online education programs, and much more.

HOW TO USE THIS BOOK

The real estate industry is continuously evolving, and it can be challenging to stay up to date on everything going on in the real estate world. This guide will help you understand only the most essential real estate terms that are used in the business. Written by a full-time real estate broker, the book could have been the length of an encyclopedia, filled with obscure and technical terms and lengthy definitions. Instead, we purposely filled it with only the words that are used in the real estate business and made the descriptions easy to understand. This book will simplify things so that you can quickly reference any term and understand what it means. Enjoy!

TERMS

1031 Exchange: Also known as a like-kind exchange, a 1031 exchange is the swapping of one piece of property for another. This is a popular tactic for real estate investors to allow their investments to grow without being subject to capital gains tax. 1031 exchanges allow a real estate investor to sell a property and then reinvest it into another property while deferring capital gains tax.

203K Loan: A 203K loan allows individuals to finance buying a home and handling the needed repairs in the same loan. 203K loans are a type of FHA loan, and not all lenders will have this type of loan option available. However, this can be a great way to buy a fixer-upper property and build equity.

3 Cs of Credit: The 3 Cs of credit are character, capital, and capacity. Character refers to how well one uses credit, makes payments on time, and job/home security. Capital refers to any assets one owns, including real estate, investments, or savings. Capacity involves one's ability to pay back debt, which includes annual salary, current debt, family obligations, etc.

Abandonment: This is when an owner voluntarily gives up their right to a property. It could involve failing to occupy the property, failing to make payments on the property or taxes, as well as a declaration of abandonment. Each area will differ in regard to their abandonment laws.

Absorption: Also known as the absorption rate, this is a calculation that determines how long it will take to sell the homes currently on the market. In real estate, the absorption rate is used to forecast market activity and prices. The absorption rate is calculated by taking the number of sales in a month and dividing it by the number of available properties. If the rate is over 20%, then that means houses are selling fast and it is a seller's market. If the rate is under 15%, then it is known as a buyer's market, and there is more supply than demand.

Abstract of Title: An abstract of title is a summary that includes any legal activity, documents, and rulings of a specific property that would prove the owner's ability to sell the home. Whenever a title search is performed on a property, there will usually be an abstract of title to go along with it.

Abstractor: Also known as an abstractor of title, this person analyzes and researches records of abstracts of titles to prove ownership in a real estate transaction. Any time a new deed transfer or any other legal activity occurs on a property, an abstractor handles the records.

Abutting: This refers to someone whose property is next to yours. There are specific building regulations and guidelines in regard to abutting rights that vary from city to city.

Acceleration Clause: An acceleration clause is a contract stipulation that allows a lender to call a loan due in full if certain criteria are not met. Common examples that would put an acceleration clause in effect include a missed payment, failure to pay property taxes, and a lack of homeowners insurance.

Acceptance: In contract law, acceptance is the agreement of an offer by both parties.

Accredited Investor: An entity or person who has been deemed capable of handling the increased risks associated with specific investment offerings. To qualify as an accredited investor, you must have an annual income of at least 200K or 300K for joint income and have had that income over the last two years. You can also qualify by having a net worth over 1 million dollars. Accredited investors are allowed to invest in particular hedge funds, private equity opportunities, and additional investments.

Acknowledgment: Acknowledgement refers to the act of signing a document and signing voluntarily, of their own will, sometimes in front of a notary public. In real estate, this occurs when the title or deed is transferred from the grantor to the grantee.

Acre: An acre is an area of land that is exactly 43,560 square feet. Acreage is commonly used in the tax records of a property to show how much land the home has.

Ad Valorem: Ad valorem taxes are taxes imposed by local city, county, or state governments based on the assessed value of the property.

ADA (Americans With Disabilities Act): This law was enacted in 1990 and makes it illegal to discriminate against a person with a disability in terms of public accommodation, employment opportunities, communication, and access to transportation, among others. A real estate agent or owner of a property may not discriminate against those with disabilities in regard to buying, leasing, or renting real property.

Addendum: An addendum is a stipulation or addition to a legal contract or document. Regarding real estate, an addendum can include a financing or a contingency agreement, or another requirement. Addendums are common in real estate contracts to clarify closing dates or other closing requirements.

Administrator: This is a person appointed by the courts to manage and dispose of the estate of an individual. In probate real estate sales, the administrator typically decides on selling a property.

Advantages of Condo Ownership: The benefits of owning a condo include affordability compared to homes, potentially more security than a single-family home, less maintenance or maintenance covered by the community/HOA fees, and access to amenities. For example, if someone is looking for real estate in a tight-knit community with a fitness center and pool, condos are a great choice.

Adverse Possession: This is when someone utilizes someone else's land without permission, but acquires ownership of land after a period of time. For example, if a landowner accidentally overextends his fence into his neighbor's property, he may obtain the land via adverse possession, even if it was an accident. The length of time and circumstances necessary to take over the land or property will vary in different jurisdictions.

Advertising Requirements: Guidelines and regulations that dictate proper advertising in real estate. Advertising requirements include the listing agent's name, their company name, a phone number, and may not include any phrases or terms which violate fair housing laws.

Affidavit: A written declaration or statement, sworn to before someone who holds the authority to bestow an oath.

Affordable Housing: Housing units that are affordable by the section of society whose income is lower than the median household income. There are programs in different jurisdictions to allow homeownership and rental housing for lower-income persons.

Air Rights: Air rights are the legal right to develop the space above land with no intrusion by others. An example of air rights would be in New York City, where there is not much land left to develop, and so builders will purchase the air rights to allow for the development of a property.

Alternatives to Foreclosure: The three most popular options to foreclosure are loan modification, short sales, or a deed in lieu of foreclosure. A loan modification allows the owner the opportunity to lower payments to a level they can afford. A short sale allows the seller to sell the home for less than what is owed if the owner can prove hardship, and if the bank accepts the lower offer. A deed in lieu of foreclosure is when the owner transfers the title or deed to the lender.

Amenities: A property's features that make it more attractive and valuable to prospective tenants or buyers. Condominiums typically come with amenities that could include a swimming pool, security, rooftop, gym, front desk, being eco-friendly, and more.

Amortization Schedule: A detailed table showing the amount of principal and interest payments on a mortgage until the end of the loan term. In a typical amortization schedule, the initial payments are mostly applied towards the interest. When closing on a property, a buyer will typically get an amortization schedule of their payments.

Annual Percentage Rate (APR): This is the yearly rate for borrowing on a mortgage or loan. This allows consumers to compare rates between different lenders easily.

Antitrust Laws: Antitrust laws are competitive market laws that were put in place to protect consumers from unethical or illegal business practices involving a lack of competition. In regard to real estate, they are laws that prohibit group boycotting, price-fixing, the allocation of markets or customers, monopolies, and tie-in agreements. The Federal Trade Commission, Department of Justice, and other real estate organizations enforce these laws.

Appraisal Process: An appraisal process is the professional estimate of the value of a property. For example, lenders require an appraisal before they will grant a mortgage and will do their evaluation of a property's value based on recent sales, the property condition, and the current real estate market.

Appraised Value: An appraised value is provided by an appraiser, which determines an estimated value of the real property at a specific moment in time. Appraisal values can vary depending on the market value of homes, as well as the demand for homes in your neighborhood. If the appraised value is lower than the contract price, then the buyer might be able to negotiate a lower price with the seller.

Appurtenances: Appurtenances are anything that is attached to a piece of property that is passed on when the property is sold. Examples of appurtenances are things like garages, water tanks, and furnaces.

Arbitration: This refers to the settling of a dispute by a third party. Arbitration is typically quicker than a traditional trial, and in most cases, it is a binding decision.

Area of Competence: Area of competence is the market, industry, or subject where one shows a certain level of expertise. In real estate, an agent with a history of residential sales can claim that real estate is an area of competence. They are not able to claim an area of competence in commercial real estate if they've only done residential sales.

Area Preference: Area preference is that specific locations are more desirable than others, and real estate can not be moved. An example of area preference is that a buyer wants to live in a particular neighborhood next to a metro, and they only have the homes in that neighborhood to choose from.

AREAA: AREAA is the Asian Real Estate Association of America, a trade organization dedicated to promoting Asian-American homeowners and real estate professionals. Founded in 2003, the AREAA advocates on the local, state, and national levels to remove barriers to homeownership for Asian American families.

ARM Loan: ARM means an Adjustable Rate Mortgage, which refers to a loan with variable interest rates that can fluctuate depending on the market rate. These loans typically have a lower initial interest rate than a fixed-rate mortgage, and then after the rate period ends, the interest rate on the loan moves to the current index. Typically, adjustable-rate mortgages are for 3 or 5 years, although depending on the lender, they can vary widely in length.

Arm's Length Transaction: An arm's length transaction is when the buyer and the seller both act in their self-interest without the interference or pressure from another party. In real estate, the buyer tries to pay the least for a home, and the seller is trying to maximize their sale price. A non-arm's length transaction would be when the buyer and seller have an existing relationship and an identity of interest. For example, when a family member sells a property to another family member, then that would not be an arm's length transaction, and it would be best to consult a CPA about the best way to transfer the property.

As Is: An "as is" listing is a property in which the buyer is purchasing the property in its current condition without any repairs from the seller. Sometimes, as-is homes are offered at a significant discount compared to other homes in good shape because they need updating.

Asbestos: Asbestos is a material that was used in homes before 1980 in flooring, insulation, and roofing and siding materials. It turned out to be a severe health hazard and was banned. In older houses, asbestos is not uncommon, and you should work with your home inspector to come up with the best course of action. Often, as long as the asbestos is not disturbed and floating in the air, then it is not a direct health threat.

Asking Price: The price at which a seller is offering their property for sale. Eventually, the selling price may be reduced after negotiation with the buyer, or in some cases, the selling price might go higher than the asking price if there is a bidding war.

Assemblage: This is when two or more adjoining lots are made into one large tract and sold together. An example of this would be if a developer bought a couple of adjacent single-family lots and combined them to build an apartment or condo building. When the highest and best use of the properties is not being met, assemblage can be a good option.

Assessed Value: In real estate, the assessed value is the valuation placed on a property for purposes of taxation by a public tax assessor. The assessed value is more of a general assessment, which is in the ballpark of the real value but not 100% accurate. The lender just wants to make sure the property is worth at least the amount the buyer is paying for it.

Assignment: This is a type of real estate transaction where the original purchaser of the property (assignor) sells the rights of that purchase contract to an end buyer (assignee) for an assignment fee. The original purchaser does not actually close on the property. This type of transaction is most common in real estate investment deals where the original buyer would assign their rights on a discounted real estate deal to another investor and make a profit just for finding the deal.

Associate Broker: This is a licensed broker, the license of whom is held under another broker. He or she is considered to be a real estate broker but is still supervised by and works for another broker similar to the way an agent would. Becoming an associate or principal broker requires a minimum of usually 3 years of experience as a full-time agent and additional continuing education requirements.

Assumption Clause: An assumption clause is a contract stipulation that allows a home seller to transfer their mortgage to the buyer. For example, in an assumption clause, the buyer essentially takes over the mortgage of a home. Assumption clauses are an attractive option if the original mortgage interest rate is lower than the current interest rates in addition to the fact the buyer will save transaction costs by not having to get a new mortgage. The majority of mortgages have a due on sale clause if the property is transferred since they do not want an unknown buyer taking over the loan. However, there are specific types of loans, including VA, FHA, and USDA loans that allow for assumptions so long as the new purchaser meets specific creditworthiness criteria.

Attorney in Fact: An attorney in fact is a person who is authorized to perform business-related transactions on behalf of someone else. An example is a person that owns a home in a different state. Instead of traveling to that state to handle all the necessary paperwork, they authorize a friend or associate (who lives in that state) to handle the paperwork.

Automated Underwriting System: A technology-driven underwriting method that offers a computer-generated loan decision. This process is becoming more common in the mortgage industry to streamline loan applications and approvals. It is also popular for applications for credit cards, personal loans, and car loans.

Avulsion: A real estate legal term which means a loss or separation of land due to water. Similar to erosion, if a river overflows and washes away a section of the land, this would be an example of avulsion.

Backup Contract: A backup contract refers to an additional contract after an original contract has been accepted. In real estate, sellers may accept backup offers, which could be higher or have better terms than the initial offer. A seller would take a backup contract to put pressure on the original offer to close on time and to have additional security in case the first offers fall through for any reason.

Balloon Mortgage: This is a mortgage for which the final payment is larger than the other payments. These types of loans are more common in shorter-term loans and are sometimes payment-free until the lump sum payment at the end. Investors often rely on balloon mortgages that allow them to finance the development of a property and sale of a property over a 12-month term, for example.

Baseboard Electric Heat: This is heat generated by electric baseboard heaters that work on a per-room basis. They are easy to install since they don't require ductwork and are quiet and inexpensive compared to central heating.

Bi-Weekly Mortgage Payment: A kind of mortgage loan where payments are made every two weeks instead of monthly. The payment is exactly one half of the monthly payment amount and can save a buyer a significant amount of interest throughout the loan. The borrower will be making one additional mortgage payment throughout the year, which does not sound like a lot but will add up to significant interest savings. This tactic can pay the mortgage off years earlier than a traditional mortgage payment. Bi-weekly mortgage payments can be set up before the buyer gets the loan, or a buyer can simply make an additional mortgage payment every week.

Bilateral Agreement: In a bilateral agreement, two parties involved in a transaction have come to an agreement. In regard to real estate, an example would be a ratified contract between the buyer and the seller, where the buyer agrees to buy at the specific price and terms, and the seller agrees to sell at the particular price and terms.

Blanket Mortgage: Also known as a blanket loan, a blanket mortgage is a loan meant for more than one property. For example, blanket mortgages are popular with real estate developers who might purchase large pieces of land and then subdivide them to be sold one at a time. Developers can often save on costs by having one blanket mortgage instead of several individual mortgages for each property.

Blighted Property: Legal term for a property that is in an unsafe, unsightly, and dilapidated condition. Different criteria are used by different states to determine whether a property should be classified as blighted. Often, blighted properties will be taxed at a higher rate to incentivize the owners to take action on the home.

Blockbusting: This is the discriminatory and illegal practice of helping minority or ethnic individuals into predominantly non-ethnic areas, and then utilizing scare tactics to compel present neighborhood residents to sell their houses at depressed prices.

Blue-Sky Laws: These are state laws that protect investors against securities fraud. They require issuers of securities, including some real estate investment opportunities, to register their offerings and provide financial details and disclosures of the deal.

Bona Fide: A legal term that refers to any situations, actions, or persons that are in good faith, honest, and without fraud. In real estate, a bona fide purchaser would be someone who buys a property without any claims or irregularities against the title.

Bonus to Selling Agent (BTSA): This is when a listing agent will offer an additional incentive for their property. It's a bonus compensation above the commission to an agent who brings a buyer to the transaction.

BPO: A broker price opinion (BPO) is similar to a real estate appraisal; the broker is typically hired by a bank or company to give their opinion for the value of a property. BPOs are common when a bank needs a valuation to list an REO or foreclosure property.

Branch Office: A branch office is an office in a different location from the main office. In real estate, a broker may have their main office in Dallas, with branch offices in Arlington, Grapevine, and other cities. Branch offices must still have a managing broker overseeing the real estate operations.

Breach of Contract: A breach of contract is a failure to complete one or several terms within the agreement. For example, if a seller decides to accept a better offer on their home after a deal has been made, the seller could be in breach of contract. It is best to consult a lawyer or your title company if you think there has been a breach of contract.

Bridge Loan: It's a short-term loan usually at higher interest rates, which can help a borrower buy another home before they sell their current residence. This "bridge" gives the borrower more flexibility in a competitive real estate market, and the loan is typically secured against their existing property.

Brownfields: A brownfield can define two different things: either a previously developed piece of land that is no longer in use, or a piece of land that is environmentally unsafe or contaminated. An example of a brownfield would be a barren strip of land where a chemical factory once was.

Buffer Zones: These are neutral, vacant areas where any real estate development is prohibited. Examples of buffer zones include small grassy areas in between commercial buildings and nature conservation areas. Buffer zones create a space between different types of properties.

Builder Warranty: This is a type of warranty that is issued to purchasers of new construction properties that typically lasts anywhere from 1 to 2 years for the home's workmanship and up to 10 years for major structural elements.

Building Codes: A comprehensive set of rules that control construction standards of buildings, including materials used, design, remodeling, repair, and other similar factors. Additionally, these regulations are the minimum requirements to ensure the safety and well-being of the building's occupants. The building codes will vary from city to city.

Bundle of Rights: In real estate, the bundle of rights refers to the legal privileges afforded to a buyer when they have purchased a property. Examples of a bundle of rights include the right of possession, the right of exclusion, and the right of disposition, the right of enjoyment, and the right of control.

Buy-Down: This is when the buyer will get a lower interest rate for the first few years of their mortgage and possibly its entire life. Payment is made to the lender by a seller, buyer, third party, or some combination of these, which allows the lender to the lower interest rate during the early years of a loan. Usually, the buy-down is applicable for the first 1 to 5 years of a mortgage. A buy-down can make the property more affordable to a potential buyer.

CAN-SPAM Act: CAN-SPAM stands for Controlling the Assault of Non-Solicited Pornography and Marketing Act of 2003. The CAN-SPAM Act applies to just about every type of business, including real estate, and it was set up to protect consumers from unsolicited emails. In regard to real estate, brokers and agents must follow the guidelines of CAN-SPAM, which include the following. Marketing emails must consist of accurate information, the subject lines must reflect the contents, a mailing address must be included, and your subscribers must be able to opt out of emails easily.

Canvassing: A useful method for real estate agents or real estate investors to generate new business. The idea is to visit property owners, appraisers, brokers, and all types of industry professionals, and begin a conversation with them, trying to form relationships. Canvassing often includes door-knocking in a particular neighborhood and leaving information about your services.

Cap Rate: A cap rate (or capitalization rate) is used in commercial real estate to determine the expected rate of return on investment. Calculating the cap rate is done by dividing the net operating income by the market value of a property. For example, if the NOI (net operating income) is $35,000, and the value of the property is $500,000, the cap rate is 7 percent.

Capital Gains Tax: Capital gains tax is a tax on the profit from the sale of an asset such as real estate or stocks. The capital gains tax in real estate allows sellers to exclude up to 250K of gains on real estate for single persons and up to 500K of gains for married couples that file jointly. However, the IRS does impose certain restrictions that you should consult your CPA about. Some of these restrictions include that the property must have been your principal residence, that you lived in the home for at least 2 of the previous 5 years, that you did not acquire the property through a 1031 exchange, and other restrictions.

Carbon Monoxide: An odorless, colorless, and tasteless flammable gas that can be harmful to humans and other animals at a high enough concentration. In real estate, common occurrences of carbon monoxide poisoning include faulty water heaters and furnaces. There should be carbon monoxide detectors throughout every house that has gas utilities or any type of gas appliances.

Cash on Cash Return: Refers to a rate of return used often in real estate transactions, which calculates the cash income received on the cash invested in a real estate property. This metric is typically used to evaluate commercial real estate investment performance or rental properties. The formula for calculating the cash on cash return is taking the net income and dividing it by the total cash invested.

Cashier's Check: A form of payment that is generally used for larger transactions such as real estate closings because it offers a more speedy and secure payment option. The money is drawn from your bank account, and a cashier or teller signs the check. The reason for using a cashier's check is that you would not have to carry around large amounts of cash, and since the money is verified by the bank, the check is guaranteed not to bounce.

Casualty Insurance: This is a broad type of insurance that can protect against personal injuries, property damage, vehicle insurance, theft, and more. Property and casualty insurance are typically packaged together into a single insurance policy. Before closing on a property, your lender will require insurance to be put in place.

Caveat Emptor: Often translated into "let the buyer beware," caveat emptor is a legal principle that states a buyer is the sole party responsible for checking and observing the quality of a product or service before a purchase is made. In real estate, when a buyer is finding a house, the responsibility is on the buyer to inspect the quality of the home and find any potential repairs or damage. Some states are "caveat emptor" states, and some states put more burden on the seller to disclose any defects.

Chain of Title: The chain of title illustrates the ownership record of a property. Since homes can date back 100+ years, the chain of title is essential to ensure there are no discrepancies in the past ownership of property. When closing a property, the title company will do the chain of title research to ensure that the property can be sold.

Change Orders: This is work that is added to or removed from the original scope of work. Change orders are common in renovation projects on a property and can lead to delays and additional costs. Although they are almost impossible to prevent, the best way to avoid change orders is to develop a specific scope of work for your contractor and project.

City Planning Commission: They are responsible for overseeing the regulations and growth of a jurisdiction. This planning includes residential, commercial, traffic, safety, and more. Sometimes, the city planning commission members are elected, and other times they are appointed by the local government.

Civil Rights Act of 1866: The Civil Rights Act of 1866 was the first significant citizenship law passed in the United States. Effectively, the 1866 law stated that all American citizens had equal rights. In regard to real estate, it meant that discrimination based on the sale, lease, or use of a property was now illegal.

Civil Rights Act of 1968: This is also known as the Fair Housing Act of 1968. This law was a follow-up to the

Civil Rights Act of 1964 and updated the Civil Rights Act of 1866 in regard to fair housing. The act further prohibited discrimination in housing, lending, as well as real estate advertising.

Clean Water Act: Passed in 1972, the Clean Water Act is designed to regulate the discharge of sewage and other pollutants into the country's bodies of water. In regard to real estate, these laws pertain to runoff during construction as well as sewage into neighboring lakes.

Clear Title: A property with a clear title means that it does not have any liens from lenders or claims to ownership in court. When a buyer purchases a property, the title company will do their due diligence to ensure that there is a clear title before closing.

Client: A client has a contractual relationship with a real estate agent. The agent is the representative of the client in the purchase or sale of a property and has signed either a listing agreement or a buyer's agent agreement.

Closing Disclosure: A closing disclosure is a five-page form that gives the final details concerning a mortgage loan. Your lender is required to provide you with this form at least 3 business days before closing so that you can make sure that all the numbers match up and that the original loan estimate you received was accurate. The closing disclosure includes loan terms, monthly payments, and closing costs.

Cloud on Title: Any defect or irregularity in a title that may deem a property unfit for sale. Examples include a lien, lawsuit, encumbrance, or other issue and are usually found during a title search. Title companies will work with a buyer and seller to get any potential clouds on the title resolved.

CMA: A Comparative Market Analysis (CMA) is the method that is used for homeowners to learn their property's current home value; it is an in-depth analysis of a home's worth. When a real estate agent is listing a home, they will first show a prospective seller a CMA of what they think the house could sell for.

Co-Ownership: Co-ownership is when several people own interest in a real estate property. There are different ways to co-own a property, including joint tenancy, tenancy in common, and tenancy by the entirety. If you are considering buying a property with someone else, it is best to consult with a title company and your CPA on the most advantageous form of co-ownership.

Coastal Zone: A coastal zone is an area by a waterway that often has additional protection and development restrictions. In 1972, Congress passed the Coastal Zone Management Act to help preserve and manage the country's coastal areas. Each jurisdiction will have different rules and regulations in regard to owning a home in a coastal zone.

Collateral: Collateral is the promise of property or other assets to secure financing. For example, land or a second property can be used as collateral when a borrower tries to obtain a new mortgage.

Collusion: Collusion is the act of cooperating in a conspiracy-like manner. In real estate, agents who attempt to manipulate offers or terms with another real estate professional to create a favorable commission would be in collusion.

Commercial Property: This is a property that is zoned and used for business. It could include office buildings, shopping centers, retail stores, and even land that has been designated as commercial zoning.

Commingling: Commingling is the illegal act of mixing a client's real estate escrow funds with personal funds. In some extreme cases of commingling, a fiduciary can be appointed to oversee an account if there is enough evidence of commingling.

Commission Split: This is the percent of commission that goes to the agent in a transaction versus the brokerage. Many real estate brokerages will have 80/20, 90/10, or even 50/50 commission splits depending on who sourced the lead. If the brokerage provided the lead for the deal, then typically an agent would split the eventual commission 50/50 with the brokerage. If the agent found the deal themselves, then they typically get a majority of the deal, depending on their brokerage agreement.

Common Areas: Common areas are places on a property which are owned by all of the owners of a property. You would find common areas in condo or co-op buildings where the residents are all able to use the common areas equally. Common areas would include the lobby, elevators, laundry rooms, rec areas, and more.

Common Law: Common law is a set of rules that are based on legal precedents, where no statutes or laws exist.

Community Property: In real estate, community property is any property owned by a married couple that was acquired during the marriage. These laws are in place in nine different states and vary slightly from state to state.

Comparables: Also referred to as comps, comparables are used to determine the value of a property by comparing homes with similar characteristics and in the same area. For example, when a buyer wants to make an offer on a home, the real estate agent will provide comps to show the values of similar homes.

Competent Parties: These are people who are legally capable of entering into a sales contract. This would include an owner or representative of an estate, someone that is legally an adult, someone that is not under the influence, and someone that is not mentally ill.

Concession: A discount or benefit offered by the seller or buyer to assist in selling a house and closing a deal. These are generally specified during negotiations and are included in closing costs.

Condemnation: In real estate, condemnation is the seizure of private property for public use in exchange for compensation. While eminent domain illustrates the state's right to seize property, condemnation refers to the actions of taking property.

Conditional Use: A conditional use permit allows a property owner to use their land or property in a fashion that is not otherwise permitted by zoning laws. An example of conditional use is operating a food truck or service shop in one's backyard.

Condo Conversion: The process of dividing real estate property held under one title into individually owned units that share common elements like a lobby, exterior walls, recreational facilities, etc. The condo conversion process will vary from city to city, and most properties will need special zoning to be able to convert them from a single property to a larger condo building.

Condo Docs: A variety of documents that establish a condominium and regulate living in a condominium community. The condo docs describe things like the location of the condo, responsibilities of the unit owners, budget, and more. A potential buyer will typically have several days to review the condo docs of a property before proceeding with a purchase.

Condominium: More commonly referred to as a condo, condominiums are private residences inside of a larger building. The individual sale of a condominium is what makes them different from apartments, which can only be rented. Condo owners share amenities in a building such as a gym, elevators, outdoor areas, and any other amenities. The condo fee and amenities will vary drastically from condo building to condo building.

Confidentiality: Confidentiality is the act or state of keeping information private and is one of the fiduciary duties required of real estate agents. The agent must not disclose any confidential information about the client that could be damaging to their negotiation.

Conflict of Interest: A conflict of interest occurs when an agent's personal or professional interest works in contrast to a client's. One of the most common examples of where conflicts of interest occur is in a dual agency scenario. Dual agency is when the agent represents both the seller and a buyer in the same transaction.

Conforming Loan: A conforming loan is a mortgage loan that does not exceed the conforming loan limit set by Freddie Mac and Fannie Mae. The conforming loan limit is adjusted every year to reflect the changes in US house prices. A mortgage loan of less than $484,350 is considered to be a conforming loan; however, in high-cost cities, the amount is higher.

Construction Loans: Construction loans are short-term loans that are used for building a home or building several properties. Both developers and homeowners looking to build a custom home could utilize a construction loan. Since these loans are riskier than a conventional mortgage, they typically have higher interest rates than a standard mortgage loan.

Contingencies: In real estate, contingencies are criteria that need to be met for the transaction to be completed. For example, most traditional offers will have a home inspection contingency that gives the buyer the right to negotiate or walk away from the transaction without penalty. There are also financing contingencies, appraisal contingencies, and even home sale contingencies.

Contract for Deed: This is when a buyer agrees to pay the seller's monthly mortgage payments without going through a lender. Then, once the payments have been made or the buyer can qualify for a traditional loan, the buyer will take the deed and ownership of the property. A contract for deed would be attractive to a buyer who would not be able to traditionally qualify for a loan through a lender. A seller would be interested in this type of transaction because they could make a profit on the financing and have many more potential buyers.

There is the risk that the buyer could stop making payments, and it is always advised to talk with a real estate lawyer in regard to this type of transaction.

Conversion: In real estate, conversion is the misappropriation of funds or property. A typical example would be if a real estate agent used a buyer's escrow funds for their own personal use.

Cooperative Ownership: In cooperative or co-op ownership, owners don't own real estate but are considered shareholders in a corporation. The corporation holds the title to the property and grants the right for residents to live in their units and to use the common elements of the co-op. Co-ops are popular in New York City and many other urban areas.

Cost Approach: A valuation method in real estate based on the premise that the price a buyer should pay for a property should equal the cost to construct an equivalent building. In this approach, the market price of a property is equal to the cost of land plus the cost of construction, less depreciation.

Cost to Cure Method: The cost to cure method is the amount of money required to restore something to new or normal working order. For example, if the shingles on the house are falling off and the cost to cure is $4,000, then the cost to cure is that amount.

Counteroffer: A counteroffer is an offer made in response to an offer from another party. For example, if you receive an offer on your house for $100,000, but you reply with an offer to sell for $110,000, then the latter is a counteroffer. The contract is not binding until both parties accept the terms in the counteroffer.

Covenant Against Encumbrances: This is a covenant that there are no encumbrances that would hinder a property owner's ability to sell or transfer title. Examples of these encumbrances could include liens, mortgages, easements, or other interests.

Covenant of Further Assurance: A covenant of further assurance means that the grantor will be responsible for any additional paperwork required to fix the title for the grantee. In other words, if something is found in the title that challenges its validity, a covenant of further assurance places the onus on the seller.

Covenant of Quiet Enjoyment: Similar to a covenant of warranty, quiet enjoyment ensures that a seller is responsible for any third-party claims. It means that the owner or tenant will be able to live in the property in peace, without interruption from outside claimants.

Covenant of Seisin: This is an Old English term which states that someone has full ownership and title of real property. It also says that there are no claims or restrictions that are not otherwise stated on the property.

Covenant of Warranty: This covenant is synonymous with quiet enjoyment and assures that any title claims would be the responsibility of the seller.

Crawl Space: It is essentially a hollow area that is found under some homes between the first floor and the ground floor. Usually, it is roughly anywhere between 1 and 3 feet high – which is high enough for somebody to enter by crawling, as the name implies. Crawl spaces allow home inspectors to check for any damage and give contractors access to plumbing, insulation, and electrical.

Credit History: Credit history is the record of an individual's past financial history in regard to credit cards, car payments, or any other types of loans. Typical credit history reports include payment history, any accounts in collections, closed accounts, and the amount of credit used. When purchasing a property, it's essential to have a solid credit history and build up your credit score as much as possible before applying for a loan so that you can get the best rate.

Credit Union: This is a financial cooperative developed by and for its members who are its borrowers, shareholders, and depositors. Being non-profit in nature, credit unions provide many banking services like commercial and consumer loans, guaranties, and credit cards, among others. Some people prefer credit unions over a traditional bank because they can offer lower rates, and they have more of a personalized and community feel to them.

Creditor: A creditor is a person or institution that extends credit to another person or entity with the idea that they will be paid back in the future. Creditors make money on the interest that they charge on the loan or credit. Some examples of creditors would be banks that make mortgages, credit card companies, car financing companies, and other similar institutions.

Curb Appeal: A term used to describe the general attractiveness of a piece of real estate property from the sidewalk to prospective buyers. When buying or selling a property, even if the house is nice on the inside, the first impressions of the curb appeal is everything.

Custom Builder: Someone who develops a building for a specific owner, designing the property to cater to said owner's requirements, instead of building first and looking for a buyer afterwards. Custom builders are typically more expensive than a traditional builder, and the prospective buyer is more involved in the process.

Customer: A customer is someone who is looking to buy real estate but is not represented by a real estate agent. There is no agency relationship with a customer, so a real estate agent typically would not do all of the work that they would with a client.

DBA: This means "doing business as," and some companies have a name that is different than their legal, registered name. Depending on the state, these companies might have to register their DBA name. For example, a company could be called "ABC Homebuyers" in the business filings but go by a name such as "Speedy Homebuyers."

Debt-to-Income Ratio: A personal finance measure that compares the debt payment of an individual to their overall income. It is a way for mortgage lenders to measure the ability of an individual to repay debts and manage monthly payments. Lenders prefer to see debt-to-income ratios under 43% because anything higher than that suggests that they are significantly more likely to have trouble making payments.

Deed in Lieu of Foreclosure: This is where a borrower surrenders the property's deed to the lender to satisfy a loan, which is in default so that they can avoid foreclosure proceedings. A deed in lieu of foreclosure is often a last resort for a homeowner who will not be able to keep their house. This arrangement saves both the owner from getting foreclosed on and saves the bank time and money that it would take them to go through foreclosure proceedings.

Deed of Trust: This is a legal document utilized in various states in lieu of a mortgage. Here, a neutral trustee holds the title of the property until the home is paid off. During the repayment period of the mortgage, the borrower is still the legal owner, and the trustee will convey the deed once the house is paid off. Some states are deed of trust states, and some are mortgage states.

Deed Restrictions: Similar to covenants, restrictions in a deed can also include various uses of the home that may not be allowed. Deed restrictions can be found in places such as historic districts, homeowners associations, or previous owners. A title company will determine what, if any, deed restrictions a property might have. Although deed restrictions are somewhat uncommon, typical deed restrictions could regulate things like the use of your home as a business, the number of trees you can remove from a property, building height, the number of vehicles allowed in a driveway or front of the house, and other similar issues.

Deed: A deed is a written, signed legal document that signifies ownership of real property. Whenever someone buys a home, the deed is transferred to reflect this change in ownership.

Defeasance Clause: A defeasance clause stipulates that the borrower will receive the title after the home loan is paid in full. In other words, once the house has been paid off, the defeasance clause will give the homeowner full ownership and the title.

Deferred Maintenance: Deferred maintenance is when repairs are postponed on a property to save costs. For example, if a property needs a yearly heat and air checkup, and the owner deferred this, at some point, they may have to spend much more money to replace the entire system. Properties with a lot of deferred maintenance can often be bought at a discount.

Deficiency Judgment Against a Borrower: This is a court ruling after a foreclosure which states a foreclosure sale did not produce enough funds to repay the loan. In these instances, a deficiency judgment usually results in a lien placed against the borrower for the amount of money owed. Many states do not allow deficiency judgments after a foreclosure.

Deliberate Misrepresentation:
Deliberate misrepresentation is when an agent or seller knows something to be untrue but intentionally presents the information differently. If a real estate agent states that a roof of a home was in excellent condition, but it is shown that the agent had prior knowledge of the roof failing, that is an example of deliberate misrepresentation.

Demand: In economics, demand is the principle that refers to an individual or group's desire to purchase certain goods or services. In real estate, a low supply of housing or a new major development such as a metro would cause an increase in demand, making the market a seller's market since they could command a higher price.

Density Zoning: These are zoning regulations that limit the development intensity of a property or area. The zoning would restrict how many units or what type of development is allowed for the given property.

Density zoning is typically established by local governments so that they can manage the growth of neighborhoods.

Depreciation: Depreciation is an asset's value, such as real estate decreasing over time. Real estate depreciation allows an owner to make an income tax deduction depending on their property. Always consult with your CPA, but being able to take a depreciation deduction is another reason to own rental real estate.

Designated Agent: Designated agency is when the agent representing a buyer and the agent representing a seller both work for the same real estate brokerage. However, they each independently represent the best interests of their client. Designated agency is a more beneficial type of arrangement than a dual agency, where one agent represents both the buyer and seller in a transaction.

Difference Between a Real Estate Agent and a Realtor: Both real estate agents and realtors are licensed to sell real estate. However, a realtor is an agent who is part of the National Association of Realtors. A realtor must adhere to the Realtor Code of Ethics and also pay a fee to join the National Association of Realtors (NAR).

Difference Between an Appraisal and a CMA: The difference between an appraisal and a CMA is that a CMA is done by a real estate broker and an appraisal is done by a real estate appraiser. For example, when a seller is looking to sell their property, a real estate agent will send them a CMA to get an idea of value. An appraisal is typically only done when a property is under contract, and the bank requires it as part of the financing. Appraisals are more of a rough estimate of value to make sure the home is worth at least what the buyer is paying for it, while a CMA is a more specific value.

Discharged: Discharging a contract means ending a real estate contract. A couple of examples of this would be performance, where all parties fulfill their obligations and get to closing. Another example would be an assignment of a contract where someone else takes over the obligations of the contract. A third example would be mutual agreement, where both parties agree to cancel the contract.

Disclosure of Agency: A disclosure of agency provides details on the relationship between an agent and their client(s). Every state will have a different disclosure of agency form that is required for representing a buyer or seller.

Disclosure of Material Facts: Material facts are facts that, if known, can alter the decision of a buyer in a transaction. Examples of material facts include a basement that floods or a leaky roof. Each state will vary in regard to what, if any, material facts need to be disclosed to a potential buyer.

Discount Broker: A discount broker is a real estate broker that provides their services at rates below the standard market commission rates. Instead of taking the full commission from a sale, a discount broker will rebate a percent or two back to the buyer or seller in a transaction.

Discount Points: A synonym for mortgage points, discount points can be purchased by a homebuyer in exchange for a lower interest rate on their mortgage. These points are a fee that is paid upfront at closing and are tax-deductible. Often, paying 1 percent of the loan amount will reduce the APR by a quarter of a percent. Therefore, for a $100,000 loan, each point will cost $1,000, and if the initial interest rate is 5 percent, one point would reduce the rate to 4.75 percent. The points and percent can vary depending on the lender and current rates.

Distress Sale: A sale of property in a situation when the seller is under pressure to sell because of an impending foreclosure, inherited property, a house in bad condition, or other issues. Usually, the property is sold at a price lower than what its present market value is and, many times, it is sold to a cash buyer who can close quickly.

Do Not Call Registry: Also known as the Do Not Call list, this is a national database of phone numbers that do not want to receive business or telemarketing calls. In regard to real estate, an agent can get fined or potentially even sued for calling numbers on the Do Not Call list.

DOM (Days on Market): It indicates the number of days a particular property has been for sale on the market. The more days on the market for a property, the more likely that home is overpriced and could be open to negotiation.

Dominant Tenement: A dominant tenement is a piece of property that benefits from an easement. An example of a dominant tenement would be if a homeowner needed to cross through their neighbor's yard to reach the park. The neighbor would grant an easement to the homeowner who owns the dominant tenement.

Double Closing: This refers to the process of a simultaneous purchase and sale of a property involving a seller, investor, and a final buyer. A double closing is similar to a traditional closing, except for the fact that it happens much faster than a standard sale. Double closings are common in real estate investment deals. The way it works is that a seller will sell the property to an investor who closes on the home and then, within a couple of hours or days, will immediately sell the property to a new investor. If an investor gets a great deal and does not want to do the work associated with fixing it up, then they would consider doing a double close.

Down Payment: This is what a buyer has to bring in cash to buy a property. The percent down a buyer needs for a down payment varies drastically and ranges from zero percent to 3.5%, 5%, 10%, 20%, and other options. It is best to talk with a few local lenders to go over your options as a homebuyer.

Dual Agency: Dual agency is when a real estate agent represents both the seller and the buyer in a real estate transaction. Several states have made dual agency illegal. In a dual agency scenario, full written disclosure of the risks associated with dual agency is required to be signed by both the seller and buyer.

Due Diligence: Due diligence in real estate is the practice of research or investigation of a property before signing a purchase contract. Some parts of due diligence would include running comparable sales on the value of similar properties, researching a specific neighborhood, and doing a thorough home inspection of a house.

Due on Sale Clause: This is a clause giving a lender the right to require that the remaining balance of a mortgage be paid in full upon a home sale or transfer of ownership. The due on sale clause is in most mortgage contracts as a means to deter a homeowner from transferring their loan to a new buyer without going through the bank.

E & O Insurance: Errors and Omission Insurance (E & O) is professional liability insurance. In regard to real estate, E and O insurance provides liability coverage in the event a broker or agent demonstrates negligence or inadequate service to a client.

Earnest Money Deposit: Earnest money is a sum deposited into an escrow account to demonstrate a willingness to buy a home. When a buyer goes under contract, most contracts will stipulate that the buyer must deposit an earnest money deposit with the title company within a few days. Most earnest money deposits are 1-3% of the sales price, and the earnest money deposit will go towards the buyer's closing costs and down payment. If the buyer backs out of the contract before their contingencies have expired, then they will receive their full earnest money deposit back.

Easement Appurtenant: This type of easement involves two properties owned by different people and allows the use of adjoining properties or land. An example of this is when a property owner needs to walk through the property of their neighbor to reach a destination, such as a beach.

Easement in Gross: An easement in gross is an easement which provides a right to use another person's land. The easement attaches to the individual or entity and not the actual property. For example, if there is an easement in gross with Bill the neighbor to use a path in the woods to access the property, then those rights are not automatically passed on to the next owner.

Easement of Necessity: This is a court-ordered easement where using a neighbor's land is absolutely necessary. As an example, if a home is landlocked and the only way a property owner or visitor can access a public road is by driving through a neighbor's property, an easement of necessity would be in place. Easements by necessity last only so long as the conditions necessary to require an easement exist.

Easements: Easements are a legal right to use someone else's land for a specific purpose without possessing it. An example of an easement would be granting the electric company to use your property to run power lines.

ECOA: ECOA is an acronym for the Equal Credit Opportunity Act. Passed in 1974, the ECOA protects consumers from unlawful discrimination in regard to obtaining loans or other forms of credit.

Economic Obsolescence: Economic obsolescence happens when a property value decreases due to external factors. A couple of examples of this would be if a freeway is built right next to a neighborhood or flight patterns change to going over a house.

Elements to a Valid Deed: There are five elements to a valid deed. The first is consideration, which means there is something of value exchanged. The second is execution, which means there will have to be signatures by both buyer and seller. The third is the description of the property or, in other words, the address or another form of property or land description. The fourth is that the names of the grantor and grantee must clearly identify who is buying and who is selling the property. The fifth is the voluntary delivery and acceptance of the property.

Eminent Domain: This is the governmental right to acquire privately owned property for public use under condemnation proceedings after payment to the owner of market value. An example of this would be when a local city needs to expand the highway and acquires properties along the path of the future highway.

Empty Nesters: A term, in general, used to indicate parents whose children have left the house after growing up.

Encroachments: In real estate, encroachments occur when a property owner builds onto a neighbor's property. For example, if a homeowner was building a fence and crossed into their neighbor's property, that would be a form of encroachment. Ordering a survey is the best way to ensure that there are no encroachments on the property you are purchasing.

Encumbrance: A mortgage, lien, liability, or claim attached to a property. It is any interest in or right to a property that may exist in someone other than the particular owner, but which won't prevent the transfer of the fee title.

Enforcement of the ECOA: The Federal Trade Commission enforces the Equal Credit Opportunity Act. The FTC ensures that no one is discriminated against based on their race, sex, gender, national origin, or religion in regard to obtaining financing.

Enforcement of the FFHA: The Fair Housing Act is enforced by HUD, also known as the United States Housing and Urban Development. The HUD Department has the authority to administer and enforce fair housing laws.

EPA: The Environmental Protection Agency began operation on December 2, 1970, and was enacted to monitor and regulate the environmental impact citizens and businesses had on the environment. Other laws passed after the establishment of the EPA include the Energy Policy Act and the Pollution Prevention Act.

Equity: This is the difference between the amount still owed on the property's mortgage and other liens, and its fair market value. For example, if the value of your property is $300,000 and you owe $200,000, then you would have $100,000 in equity.

Escalation Clause: In real estate, an escalation clause means a prospective buyer has placed an offer that escalates above their initial asking price should another bidder make an offer higher than the original offer. For example, a buyer could make an offer of $150,000, with an escalation clause to $175,000 if they think there will be multiple offers. If the seller decides to go with the escalated amount above the initial asking price, then they have to show proof of the other offer that triggered their escalation clause to kick in.

Escheat: This is where a property is transferred to the state when no heirs, beneficiaries, or claimants to the property are available. For example, if a property owner dies and does not have a will or any legal heirs, escheat would grant ownership of the property to the State. The escheat laws vary from state to state.

Escrow Agent: An escrow agent holds the earnest money deposit and other considerations for parties during a real estate transaction until it is completed. In real estate, the title attorney is usually the escrow agent.

Estate for Years: This is a form of a lease where a tenant leases a property with a specific starting and ending date. That means that no notice to vacate is required since there is a definite ending date on the lease. If both parties agree in writing, the lease may be renewed.

Estate From Period to Period: Estates from period to period is a lease agreement that has no definite termination date, but that continues from week to week, month to month, or year to year.

Estate Tax: In federal tax law, estate taxes are levied on property and assets at their fair market value when an individual passes away. For example, if the deceased has assets valued at $10 million, estate taxes would apply at the market value even if the deceased paid less at the time of purchase. Estate taxes are only paid by the wealthiest estates when the value typically exceeds over 5 million dollars, although it will vary depending on the state.

Estates at Sufferance: This is when a tenant occupies a property after their lease has expired, without the permission of the landlord.

Estates at Will: Also known as a tenancy at will, this is an agreement where either party can terminate the lease as long as enough advance notice is given. In this instance, a tenancy at will may not require a contract, since either party can opt out at any time.

Estoppel Certificate: Also referred to as an Estoppel Letter, this is a signed statement of facts about the financial obligations in a mortgage or lease that cannot be rebuked later. With a lease, an estoppel certificate can be used with a tenant and landlord to confirm financial information about the term of the lease, amount of the lease, and other relevant information to the lease.

Et al.: This is Latin for "and others." The phrase is commonly used in legal documents, including property deeds where the deed might have "Mike Smith et al.," signifying that there are others on the deed as well.

Exclusive Agency: This is a listing agreement between a seller and a real estate brokerage that allows the real estate agent or firm to be the only agent marketing the property. However, if the seller finds a buyer on their own, they do not have to pay a commission.

Exclusive Right to Sell: This is a listing agreement that provides a real estate agent with the sole right to sell a specific property, regardless of who finds the buyer for the home. The seller has to pay the commission of the agent even if the seller finds a buyer.

Exculpatory Clause: A contract provision that offers relief to one party if there are damages caused during the execution of that contract. Typically, the issuing party of the exculpatory clause is the one looking to be relieved of potential liability. Exculpatory clauses are often found in rental agreements stating that the landlord is not responsible for any damage or injury at their property. Additionally, they are in mortgage documents that say that in the event of a foreclosure, the bank can only take the property back and not go after additional assets of the buyer.

Executor: A person whose name is mentioned in a will to manage a deceased person's estate. The court appoints an administrator if no executor is named in a will. In a probate or inherited real estate transaction, this is the person who has the power to sell or keep a property.

Express Contract: An express contract is an oral or written agreement in which all terms are decided upon and understood by both or all parties. An example of an express contract is a signed agency agreement.

Express Grant: An express grant is a form of easement that requires permission from a grantor, who must own the property in question. For example, if a neighbor wants to install a walkway that is on the owner's property for easier access to their home, they would need to ask the owner for an express grant to build the path on the other person's property.

Express Reservation: This is a type of easement when an owner splits a large piece of land into two or more pieces and creates an easement that allows the original owner to keep some rights. An express reservation easement would allow the owner to sell part of their property while still being able to access a lake or body of water.

Fair Housing Issues in Advertising: Fair housing issues in advertising include any marketing or advertisements which show preference to a specific class based on race, gender, familial status, disability, religion, or national origin. For example, a real estate advertisement saying "English speakers only" or "no wheelchairs" would be violations of fair housing.

Fair Market Value: The highest price which a buyer, willing but not forced to buy, would pay, and the lowest which a seller, willing but not forced to sell, would accept.

Familial Status: This refers to the makeup of your family and having at least one child under 18 years of age or anyone pregnant. Under FHA guidelines, landlords may not discriminate based on familial status.

Fannie Mae: Fannie Mae is the Federal National Mortgage Association, an entity sponsored by the U.S. Government that was founded during the Great Depression. Fannie Mae's purpose is to provide secure mortgage loans to help more American citizens afford homes. Fannie Mae does not offer mortgages to borrowers. However, it does guarantee them and is one of the largest purchasers of mortgages on the secondary market.

Farm Service Agency (FSA): The FSA is an agency under the United States Department of Agriculture. The FSA offers farm loans often referred to as direct farm ownership loans. Direct farm ownership loans are used to enlarge a farm or ranch, construct a new farm, or improve existing farm or ranch buildings.

Federal Fair Housing Act (FFHA) Violations: Violations of the Fair Housing Act are many and varying, and the penalty for violating FFHA regulations can be steep fines, loss of your real estate license, and more.

Federal Fair Housing Act of 1968: Also known as Title VIII of the Civil Rights Act of 1968, this act protects families and individuals from discrimination in rental, sale, advertising of housing, or financing. It prohibits discrimination based on color, disability, race, religion, sex, national origin, and family status.

Federal Insurance Office (FIO): The Federal Insurance Office was established after the financial crisis of 2008 as a means of providing financial stability. Under Title V of the Dodd-Frank Wall Street Reform and Consumer Protection Act, the FIO oversees all aspects of the insurance sector.

Federal Reserve: This is the central bank of the U.S., commonly known as the "Fed," which regulates the U.S. financial and monetary system. It's a major driving force in banking and the economy.

Federal Tax Liens: Federal tax liens are the United States' legal claim against a property when federal taxes are not paid. If a homeowner fails to pay their tax bill, the US government could put a federal tax lien on their property until payment is made.

Fee Simple Absolute: One of the two types of fee simple ownership. Fee simple is when a homeowner has unconditional ownership of their property, and this is the highest form of ownership. This type of ownership is common when someone purchases a property or receives property as a gift.

Fee Simple Defeasible: This is the other type of fee simple ownership. In fee simple defeasible, the right to ownership comes with certain conditions and, if they are not met, the property could go back to a third party.

Fee Simple: Fee simple is a type of freehold estate in which the owner of a property can use it to its fullest extent. A fee simple estate is the highest possible real estate ownership form.

FHA Loan: An FHA (Federal Housing Administration) loan is a mortgage issued by an FHA-approved lender and insured by the FHA. They require a lower down payment and lower credit score than most conventional loans. If your credit score is above 600, you only need to put down 3.5% when you are a first-time homebuyer, and the property will be your principal residence.

FHA: FHA is the Federal Housing Association. They provide mortgage insurance on loans made by FHA-approved lenders. An example of the FHA is an association that helps lenders with easy financing and low down payments.

FHFA: FHFA is the Federal Housing Finance Agency. The FHFA regulates Fannie Mae, Freddie Mac, and the Federal Home Loan Banks. The FHFA was established in 2008 to assist in strengthening the US housing finance system.

Fiduciary Duties to a Client: Fiduciary duties are legally mandated obligations that a real estate agent must abide by during a transaction for the client they are representing. These specific fiduciary duties include obedience, disclosure, loyalty, accounting, reasonable care and diligence, and confidentiality.

FIRPTA: FIRPTA stands for the Foreign Investment in Real Property Tax Act of 1980, which imposes income taxes on foreign persons or entities when they sell property in the United States.

First Mortgage: A first mortgage is a home loan, which is the primary lien on a property. When you first purchase your home, the mortgage you received to provide the initial financing would be the first mortgage. In the event of default, the first mortgage has priority over others' liens or claims on a property.

First-Time Homebuyer: An individual who is buying a principal residence for the first time. There are specific programs and loans that are designed for first-time homebuyers, including FHA loans at 3.5% and others. A first-time homebuyer should always consult with their lender and real estate agent about first-time homebuyer programs.

Fixity: Fixity means the land can not be moved to a different location, or in other words, it is fixed in location. It also refers to the fact that buildings or houses built on the land take a long period of time to pay for themselves. Fixity is one of the four economic properties of land.

Fixture: A permanent part of an apartment or a house that gets conveyed with the transfer of the real estate. If something is physically attached to the property, it is considered a fixture. Some basic examples of fixtures would include things like a chandelier, a sink, refrigerator, or other integral parts of the house. If there are any questions about what is a fixture and what conveys with the property, the buyer should ask the agent before submitting an offer to avoid confusion on the final walk-through at closing.

Flat Fee Listing: Instead of paying a real estate agent a percentage of the sale price, a Flat Fee MLS listing means the client pays a flat rate (usually a few hundred dollars) to have their listing in the multiple listing service. When a seller does a flat fee listing, the home is technically still for sale by owner since the real estate agent is only paid to put the property on the MLS.

Flood Certification Fee: A small fee charged to the buyer as part of their closing costs to receive the government-required document that helps to determine whether a property is situated in a flood plain. If the home is located in a flood plain, then the buyer will have to purchase additional flood insurance.

Flood Control Act: The Flood Control Act is one of several federal laws designated to establish levees, dams, and other flood control measures. These measures were passed after several major floods caused severe damage to major American cities.

Flood Insurance: Insurance compensating the loss by flood damage. Lenders require it for houses designated in a flood plain.

Floodplain: A floodplain is a piece of low, flat land where water pools, collects, and flows during times such as heavy rain. They are often located near a river or body of water.

Forbearance: Forbearance is an agreement between the lender and the borrower that will pause a foreclosure. If a homeowner is having financial difficulties but has always paid their mortgage on time, the lender would consider granting a forbearance, allowing the owner to get caught up on their payments and keep their house.

Foreclosure: Foreclosure is the process of a lender taking back a property due to the owner failing to make their payments on the home. Each state will have different timelines and procedures for foreclosing on a property. Most banks prefer not to initiate a foreclosure because of the cost and time involved, and if possible, they try to work out an arrangement with the seller.

Four Characteristics of Value: The 4 characteristics of value are demand, utility, scarcity, and purchasing power. Demand varies from area to area, depending on the current market trends. Utility is the idea that the property must have usefulness for a buyer in the marketplace. Scarcity is the idea that the rarer a type of property is, the more value it must have. Lastly, purchasing power is all the types of buyers that can afford a property, and the more buyers that can afford the property, the better.

Fraud: Fraud is the act of deception, which results in one party's harm and another party's gain. In real estate, one example would be a real estate agent who rents out a home that is vacant and not available for rent, such as a foreclosure.

Freddie Mac: Freddie Mac is a government-sponsored entity that buys mortgages and packages them into mortgage-backed securities, which are then sold on the secondary mortgage market. The purpose behind Freddie Mac is to increase the money supply available for mortgages and also provide guarantees for those loans.

Freehold Estate: A freehold estate is a type of ownership that grants a right to use for an indefinite period of time. This is in contrast to a less than freehold estate, which is only held for a fixed time.

Functional Obsolescence: Functional obsolescence pertains to a property that has features that are neither desirable or practical. For example, an older 750-square-foot home with only two bedrooms in a neighborhood with mostly new construction five-bedroom homes would be considered functionally obsolete.

Funding Fee: A funding fee occurs for buyers who get a VA (Veterans Administration) mortgage. Most VA loans do not require any down payment or monthly mortgage insurance payment. However, all VA loans have a one-time funding fee. If you are a first-time VA homebuyer, then the fee is 2.15% of the purchase price of the property.

General Agent: In general agency, a real estate agent is able to handle all forms of the real estate transaction, but without power of attorney. A real estate agent under general agency can submit bids, accept offers, or any other transactions as stipulated by their agency agreement.

General Contractor: A general contractor or GC oversees the construction on a project and contracts with the owner of a property to get the work done. Instead of the homeowner hiring and coordinating different contractors such as electrical, plumbing, and others, the general contractor is responsible for managing and hiring the subcontractors. A homeowner or investor typically pays more for a general contractor than if they just hired individual tradesmen separately; however, in theory, the homeowner would also have less management involved in the project.

General Lien: A general lien is a lien against all property and assets that are owned by a debtor. This is in contrast to a specific lien that is just attached to a property.

General Partnership: This is an unincorporated business entity where two individuals (or more) agree to share all profits, losses, and liabilities. For example, when two real estate investors go into a real estate investment deal together , that is a general partnership.

General Warranty Deed: In real estate, a general warranty deed demonstrates and guarantees that a seller has complete ownership of a property. A general warranty deed offers the greatest amount of protection to the purchaser of a property.

Gift Deed: A gift deed is the transfer of property ownership, which is voluntary to a friend, family member, or some other organization. For example, when someone decides to donate their home for an orphanage, a gift deed is utilized. It is always wise to consult with a CPA and real estate attorney before receiving a gift deed.

Gift Letter: A written correspondence stating explicitly that funds received from a relative or a friend are a gift. When buying a property, a lender will want to see a gift letter to know that a borrower has received financial assistance in making a down payment on a property.

Ginnie Mae: Ginnie Mae is the Government National Mortgage Association, which is a part of the

Department of Housing and Urban Development, or HUD. Ginnie Mae guarantees mortgage-backed securities, which allows mortgage lenders to offer better prices on loans to their customers.

Good and Marketable Title: This is a title that is free from any claims, liens, or other title-related issues. A seller has an implied obligation to transfer a good and marketable title to the buyer for a real estate closing. The title company handling the transaction will do their due diligence to ensure that there is a marketable title.

Good Faith Estimate: A good faith estimate, or GFE, is a document which shows estimates of mortgage payments. Good faith estimates allow prospective homebuyers the opportunity to shop with different lenders and compare rates. After 2015, two new disclosure forms replaced the good faith estimate, i.e. the loan estimate and the closing disclosure form.

Graduated Lease: A graduated lease is a flexible lease with variable payments depending on the market value of the property. For example, if the building's value increases over time, the landlord can increase the rent. These types of leases are more common on longer-term leases for commercial properties.

Grandfathered In: This refers to the continued legal use of a real estate property or modification to a property that existed before new laws and regulations were put in place. These laws will vary in every city.

Grant Deed: A grant deed is designed to transfer all interest of ownership from a seller to a buyer. A grant deed guarantees that the property has not been sold to anyone else and does not have any undisclosed liens or restrictions. This type of deed offers more protection to a buyer than a quitclaim deed and less protection than a warranty deed. Grant deeds are common in California and several other states.

Grantee: A grantee is a person or entity that receives the title to a property. The grantee is the buyer of a property.

Grantor: A grantor is a person or entity who conveys their interest in a property to another. The grantor is the seller.

Gross Lease: A gross lease is when a tenant pays a flat rental fee, which includes rent as well as taxes, insurance, and utilities. Gross leases are uncommon in residential properties but are popular with commercial properties.

Gross Rent Multipliers (GRM): This is a ratio of the property's purchase price to its annual income to determine how long it will take for the rental income to pay for the property. For example, if a GRM is 5, that means it will take 5 years of rental income for a property to be paid for. The formula for gross rent multiplier is to take the purchase price and divide that number by the gross annual rent. As an investor, the lower the gross rent multiplier, the better, since that means it will take less time to pay off the property price.

Ground Lease: A ground lease is typically a long-term commercial lease that allows the tenant to develop a piece of property at their own expense during that lease period. A couple of examples of this would be McDonalds or Starbucks building a location on a strategic site where the actual land is not for sale.

Hazard Insurance: This is insurance that protects a property owner against damage from storms, fires, earthquakes, other natural events, theft, vandalism, and more. Mortgage lenders will require hazard insurance before issuing a loan.

HECM: An HECM loan is a Home Equity Conversion Mortgage. This is a reverse mortgage for senior homeowners who have paid off their property or have a lot of equity and are currently living in the home. This type of loan is the only reverse mortgage insured by the US Federal Government, and it allows the owner to withdraw an amount of the home equity.

HELOC: A home equity line of credit, which is often referred to as HELOC, is a line of credit where the lender agrees to lend a maximum amount based on the collateral in the borrower's home. Some common purposes for using a HELOC include remodeling your house, paying for college, and even going on vacation.

HERA: HERA, which is The Housing and Economic Recovery Act, was created to address the subprime mortgage crisis of 2008. This act allowed the Federal Housing Administration (FHA) to guarantee up to $300 billion in new 30-year fixed mortgages for subprime borrowers. The purpose of the act was to restore faith in Fannie Mae and Freddie Mac by strengthening regulations and adding capital to both mortgage funding organizations.

Highest and Best Use: Highest and best use refers to the most advantageous legal use that produces maximum productivity or value of a property or land. For example, a vacant lot that is zoned for an apartment building would not be at its highest and best use until the building was developed.

HOA Docs: HOA Docs or Homeowners Association Docs are what a buyer receives when purchasing a property in an HOA community. HOA docs include information about the community, including the articles of incorporation, rules and regulations, declaration of covenants, reserve funds, and more. Once a buyer receives the HOA docs, in most states, they will have 3 days to review the information and can withdraw their offer without penalty at any time during those 3 days.

HOA Fees: HOA fees are funds used to cover the costs of services provided to an HOA community. For example, some HOAs manage the trash pickup, front yard maintenance, swimming pools, and community clubhouse. These amenities would be covered by the HOA fees, although each HOA is different. Sometimes HOA fees are paid monthly, and sometimes they are paid every quarter.

Hold Harmless: It is a statement in a legal contract describing that an organization or individual isn't liable for any damages or injuries to the individual who signs the contract. Hold harmless agreements are used in real estate when a house has mold or is in bad condition, and the potential buyer would need to sign this form before entering the property.

Holdover Tenant: A tenant that retains possession of the property after their lease has expired. If a tenant continues to pay rent after the lease agreement has expired, the landlord can either present a new lease agreement or consider them a trespasser and initiate eviction procedures.

Home Warranties: This is a policy paid by homeowners that covers the cost of repairing different home appliances and major components of a house in case they break down. It offers financial protection for homeowners who could face unexpected repairs or replacements with their property. Home warranties are relatively common, and depending on the type of warranty and size of the property, they cost around $500.

Homeowners Protection Act: Also known as the HPA, the Homeowners Protection Act is a law that was created to reduce the private mortgage insurance payment (PMI) for homeowners who are no longer required to pay it. The law stipulates that once a homeowner has acquired enough equity in their home to cover what they owe, they will automatically no longer have to pay for PMI.

Homestead Exemption: This is a legal provision that protects a property from certain creditors following the death of a spouse or bankruptcy. The homestead exemption can also give surviving spouses property tax relief.

Honest and Fair Dealing: This refers to the obligation that a real estate agent is not allowed to do anything that may hurt or injure the other party in a contract, even if it is not in writing. The agent must act with honesty and treat parties fairly in a real estate transaction.

Housing Expense Ratio: This is the percentage of your gross monthly income that is paid towards housing expenses. A lender will use this ratio to determine how much house you can afford. They will take your gross monthly income and divide it by your new mortgage payment. The threshold for most mortgage loan approvals is 28%. Lenders can accept housing expense ratios that are higher than 28% based on things like excellent credit history, a low loan-to-value ratio, and other factors.

How to Calculate Area Dimensions: Simply multiply the length of an area by its width to calculate area dimensions. For example, a room that is 10 feet by 10 feet has an area of 100 feet.

HUD Poster: Also known as the Fair Housing Poster, a HUD Poster is a poster that displays information regarding the Fair Housing Act. This poster is required to be posted in real estate brokerages and other services that are in the real estate business.

HVAC: HVAC is short for heating, ventilation, and air conditioning of a property. The HVAC system is often one of the most significant repair costs of a property, so it is always advised to get a thorough home inspection and, if needed, have an HVAC contractor fix any issues.

Hypothecation: Hypothecation is a type of collateral offered to secure a loan or other funding, but ownership remains in control of the borrower. For example, if a homeowner offers their land as hypothecation to fund the remodeling of their house, they would still own the land as long as the conditions of the agreement were met.

Immobility: Immobility is one of the three physical characteristics of land. Land cannot be moved from one area to another, and it is affected by the environment around it. The location of the land or property will have an enormous impact on its value.

Implied Agency: Implied agency is when a real estate agent gives advice or provides any service without having a formal contract. Based on the conduct of the real estate agent, it is generally implied that there is a real estate agency relationship. Many states have laws stating that no agency can exist without a written agency agreement.

Impounds: This is an account that mortgage companies maintain to collect amounts like property taxes, private mortgage insurance, hazard insurance, and other payments required from the mortgage holders. Instead of a homeowner paying a large property tax bill or additional large expense at the end of the year, the mortgage company will include these fees into the monthly payments to make sure that everything is paid.

Improvements: Improvements are permanent additions to a property that increase its capital value. An example of an improvement would be renovating a kitchen or replacing the HVAC system.

Inclusionary Zoning: Also known as inclusionary housing, these are zoning ordinances that require new construction housing developments to have a portion of the housing be affordable to low- and median-income citizens.

Income Approach: A type of real estate appraisal method where the value of a property is based on the income of the property. The income approach is more commonly used with commercial properties since it is based on the income and future income of a property.

Income Property: Property that produces income, generally from rent. Income properties can be residential or commercial, and they can be a great alternative from investing in the stock market or another type of investment.

Independent Contractor: An independent contractor is a person or business that provides services for a person or company under a verbal or written contract. Independent contractors are different from employees, and real estate agents are an example of independent contractors.

Indestructibility: Indestructibility is one of the three physical characteristics of land, and it means that a piece of land cannot be destroyed, even if everything on the land can be. An example of indestructibility is a forest fire. The houses will be destroyed, but the land will still be there, even though it will have lost value.

Installment Loans: An installment loan refers to the majority of loans extended to borrowers, where a borrower puts down a lump sum and makes payments over time. These are loans with any regularly scheduled payment or installment and include mortgages, auto loans, or personal loans.

Installment Sales: An installment sale is where the seller receives at least one payment on the property after the tax year of the sale. Installment sales are a type of seller financing and can save a seller money on the sale of their property. Always consult with a CPA before doing this type of transaction.

Insurance Value: This is the cost of rebuilding the property in the event of a fire or other catastrophe that would cause the home to need replacement. Unlike the market value, insurance value does not include the cost of buying the land and instead is only based on the amount of the materials and labor needed to rebuild the property in the same condition as it was.

Interim Financing: The process of obtaining short-term, temporary financing to close a real estate transaction. Also known as bridge financing, this type of loan is used by buyers who need to purchase a property before selling their current residence.

Intestate Succession: This happens when someone who owns property dies and no will exists. The state will distribute the property to the rightful heirs and beneficiaries. The laws about the distribution of the property vary from state to state.

Inverse Condemnation: Inverse condemnation occurs when a property is seized or damaged by the government without fair compensation. Rather than the government taking legal action in condemnation, the landowner takes legal action against the government in an inverse condemnation.

Investment Value: Investment value measures the potential value of a property based on a variety of factors, such as rental income, location, economic conditions, and more. This is different than the market value, which is done through a standard appraisal process. The investment value could be more or less than the market value, depending on the various economic factors.

Involuntary Liens: Involuntary liens are liens that can be put on a debtor's property without having to file a lawsuit. An example of involuntary liens would be property tax liens, IRS liens, child support liens, and mechanic's liens. Before a third party places a lien on the property, they must give the owner some type of notice that the action will be taking place.

IRA: An Individual Retirement Account or IRA is a tax-favored savings program that individuals use to save for retirement. A certain amount can be deposited each year in such an account, and there are several different types of IRAs, including traditional IRAs, Roth IRAs, SEP IRAs, and others. This money isn't subject to income tax for that particular year or the following years until it is withdrawn during your retirement years.

Joint and Several Liability: In legal terms, joint and several liability means that a plaintiff can hold any of multiple defendants fully liable. An example in real estate is that, if two individuals take out a mortgage for a property, each owner is responsible for the entire debt, not just their percentage share.

Joint Ownership: Joint ownership is when two or more people possess ownership of a home. The most common form of joint ownership is when a husband and wife purchase property. There are three main types of joint ownership, including tenancy in common, joint tenancy, and tenancy by the entirety.

Joint Tenancy: Joint tenancy is a type of property ownership where one or more people own real estate together. In joint tenancy, if an owner dies, their interest is transferred to any survivors without any legal interference.

Joint Venture: A joint venture is a real estate deal between multiple parties to develop a property. Joint ventures are common in real estate and can involve one party bringing the financing while another party brings the experience to a deal. Joint ventures can be set up as LLCs, corporations, partnerships, or another type of entity.

Judicial Foreclosure: A judicial foreclosure is a foreclosure case that goes through the judicial process or court system. Many states require foreclosures to go through the court system while other states are non-judicial. The reason for judicial foreclosures is to protect the borrower in the case of unscrupulous lenders.

Jumbo Loan: A jumbo loan, or a jumbo mortgage, is financing that exceeds FHFA limits. Jumbo loans are ineligible to receive guarantees or securitization from

Fannie Mae or Freddie Mac. These loans are used to finance more expensive properties and require a larger down payment and higher credit scores. Each area will have different jumbo loan limits depending on the price ranges for that city.

Junior Mortgage: A junior mortgage is any mortgage that is taken after the first mortgage. The most common type of junior mortgage would be a Home Equity Loan or Home Equity Line of Credit (HELOC). This is where the homeowner would be able to draw against the equity of the property on the difference between the first mortgage and the value of the home. Homeowners would take out a junior mortgage to pay for different expenses like home improvements, college tuition, or other reasons. Since a junior mortgage is riskier, lenders will typically charge higher interest rates than on a first mortgage. Also, in the event of a default or foreclosure, the first mortgage has priority to get paid off first, and then the second mortgage gets paid off.

Kickback: A kickback is an illegal fee paid to an agent in favor of receiving business from a vendor or client. In real estate, when a contractor pays a real estate broker to handle any home repair needs for their client's listings, they are receiving a kickback.

Latent Defect: In real estate law, latent defects are issues or problems that would not have been found in a thorough property exam. For example, rusted plumbing throughout the house that was past its useful life expectancy is a latent defect.

Lead-Based Paint: Before 1978, lead was utilized in paint to produce a better look and faster drying. However, once it was discovered how toxic lead-based paint is to humans, it was banned. Lead-based paint disclosures are required to be signed in any property built before 1978, since it is presumed that there could be lead underneath a coat of paint.

Lease Purchase: Commonly known as rent-to-own, lease purchase is an agreement where tenants may rent a property with the option to buy the house after a specified number of payments. A lease-purchase sale opens the market up for potential buyers who would not be able to traditionally qualify for a home and can also get a seller a premium price for their property. Always consult with a real estate attorney when considering doing a lease purchase as a buyer or seller.

Leasehold Estates: A leasehold estate involves a tenant who has exclusivity to a property for a fixed timeframe. An owner should always get any type of lease in writing and signed by both parties before renting out their property or land.

Legal Description: A legal description of a property is the record of the land boundaries, county, and state of where the home is located. Common forms of legal descriptions for properties include metes and bound, rectangular survey, and the lot and block systems.

Legally Competent: Being legally competent means that those who are of legal age to enter into a contract are not under the impairment of drugs or alcohol and are mentally competent. This is a requirement for a valid real estate contract.

Lender's Title Insurance: Insurance that protects the mortgage lender from any potential claims or lawsuits. Lender's title insurance is required to get a mortgage loan, and this type of insurance only protects the lender. Many buyers will also get an owner's title insurance policy, which can offer further protection in the event of a title issue.

Lessee: A lessee is the formal term to describe a tenant. For example, when a tenant is filling out a lease agreement, they will be referred to in writing as the lessee.

Lessor: A lessor is a formal term used in contracts to describe a landlord. For example, when a landlord is filling out a lease agreement, they will be referred to as the lessor.

Leverage: A finance term that means the utilization of debt (i.e. a mortgage) to purchase assets such as real estate. When a home buyer or investor puts 10% down on a property, then that would be using leverage, since they would be the 100% owner of the house.

Lien Priority: A lien priority is the order in which creditors are paid following a foreclosure. For example, in a foreclosure, a first mortgage would get paid off first, and if any funds are remaining, then a second mortgage, mechanic's lien, or another type of judgment lien would get paid off. The lien priority would decide what order creditors will be paid.

Lien Theory: In a lien theory state, the borrower holds the deed to the home, and the mortgage company places a lien on the title until the house is paid in full. When someone buys a home in a lien theory state, they technically own the home, but the lien from the mortgage company must be satisfied before they can take full ownership. There are lien theory states as well as title theory states, where a trustee holds the title to the property until the loan is completely satisfied.

Liens: Liens are a public notice on your property that you owe a creditor some money. A title company would discover any liens when a seller tries to sell their property, and the lien must be satisfied upon closing to receive clear title. There are numerous types of liens, such as tax liens, mechanic's liens, HOA liens, and others.

Life Estates: A life estate is a type of joint ownership where a parent gives their property to the children but keeps the right to own and occupy their home until their death. At that point, the ownership is automatically transferred to the child or children. Life estates can be an excellent way to avoid probate by having the property transfer to the children of an estate upon the death of a parent. Always talk with a lawyer in regard to this type of ownership.

Limited Partnerships: A limited partnership involves two or more parties, but with a different structure compared to a general partnership. In a limited partnership, the day-to-day management is handled by the general partner, while the other partners have a limited interest in the company. In regard to real estate, a developer with silent partners who finance the project is an example of a limited partnership.

Liquidated Damages: This is a clause in a real estate contract that states the amount a seller would receive if the buyer breaches the contract. Liquidated damages are typically not more than 3% of the sales price of the property.

Liquidity: Liquidity is how fast an asset or security can be bought or sold. The most liquid asset is cash and then stocks and bonds. Real estate is one of the most illiquid assets because of the time it takes to transact a closing.

Lis Pendens: In legal terms, lis pendens is a written notice of a filed lawsuit. Lis pendens are attached to the public record and would affect the sale of a property. A common form of lis pendens is when a bank initiates a foreclosure proceeding against a seller.

Listing Broker: This is a licensed real estate professional who has an agreement to list the property and get it sold. There are different types of listing agreements, ranging from flat fee services to the more common full-service commission listing.

Littoral Rights: Littoral rights are related to landowners that have land bordering large lakes and oceans. Littoral rights are concerned with the use and enjoyment of the shore, whereas riparian rights are more concerned with the use of the actual water when it is a river or stream.

Load-Bearing Wall: One of the most important structural elements that supports the weight of a structure. Anytime a buyer purchases a property and wants to tear down walls to open up space, they need to verify with a licensed contractor or engineer that none of the walls are load-bearing walls.

Loan Estimate: A three-page form that provides a borrower with important information about the loan, including monthly payment, total closing costs, and estimated interest rate for the loan, among others. This form took effect in 2015 and was created to provide clear language to help a borrower understand the total costs of the mortgage.

Loan Processing: Also referred to as mortgage processing, loan processing involves the full process of home financing, from the original application until closing. Loan processes include the home appraisal, credit check, verification of all documents and finances, and any other pertinent information.

Loan-to-Value Ratios: LTV or loan-to-value ratios are calculated by dividing the value of a property by the total amount borrowed. For example: A $100,000 property with a $20,000 down payment equals $80,000 borrowed. As a ratio, the loan-to-value is 80% or .8. The lower the loan-to-value ratio, the less risky it is for the lender. Loans with higher LTVs can often require mortgage insurance.

Lock-In Rate: This is the guarantee of a lender to provide a borrower with a specific interest rate and loan terms for a certain period of time. Since mortgage rates can change daily, it can be smart to lock in a low rate and get to closing. Rate locks are often available for 30, 45, and 60 days, depending on your lender and type of financing.

Lot and Block System: The lot and block system is a method used to describe and identify properties clearly. It is also known as the recorded plat survey system. To find and identify a property, the lot and block system uses the lot and block number, the name of the subdivision plat, and the name of the city and state.

Lowball Offer: An offer that is substantially lower than a property's asking price. In a buyer's market, a lowball offer can be an excellent way for the buyers to receive the best deal possible. Similar to any type of real estate offer, a seller can either ignore the offer, counter the offer, or accept the lowball offer.

Loyalty: Loyalty is a fiduciary duty of a real estate agent and requires that an agent maintain complete loyalty to their clients and put their clients' interests above their own.

LTV Ratio: LTV ratio means the loan-to-value ratio, and it is the ratio between the amount borrowed for the home and its assessed value. For example, a $100,000 home, minus a $15,000 down payment, means that $85,000 is borrowed, creating an LTV of 85%. The higher the percentage of the LTV ratio is, the riskier the loan will be for the lender, and they might require mortgage insurance.

Mailbox Rule: A rule of law that describes that an offer of a contract becomes effective immediately once it has been properly mailed.

Market Cycles: Market cycles are a sequence of events that are reflected in demographic, economic, and emotional factors that affect the supply and demand for property. The real estate market has historically been cyclical and follows a pattern where there is a recovery, expansion, hyper supply, and then a recession.

Market Value: Market value is what a property would sell for in an open and competitive market. A real estate agent will assist a buyer or seller out with comparable sales or "comps" to determine what they think would be a good market value for the property.

Marketable Title: A marketable title is a title for real property that is free of any title claims or defects. The title company will do a title search to make sure there is marketable title, and a purchaser of a home would not be able to close on it until there is a marketable title.

Master Plan: This is a comprehensive long-term zoning plan for a city, county, or other governmental jurisdiction. Real estate builders also utilize a master plan for a community or a planned subdivision.

Material Defects: A material defect is an issue with a property, which can hurt the value. Examples of material defects include a faulty foundation, a damaged roof, or a damaged plumbing system. Depending on the state, a seller is almost always required to disclose any material defects.

Mechanics Liens: Mechanic liens are legal documents that reserve contractors or suppliers the right to seek payment not received from the owner of a property. A contractor would put a mechanic's lien on a property if they did not receive payment for a roofing project, kitchen renovation, or many other scenarios. This lien would attach to the property and put a public notice on the title that would have to be resolved before closing on the home.

Meeting of the Minds: In contract law, a meeting of the minds means that two parties are in agreement with each other. In real estate, once a buyer and seller came to a meeting of the minds, they can sign the purchase and sale contract.

Megan's Law: Megan's Law is a federal law which requires that all states provide public information regarding the whereabouts of sex offenders. In regard to real estate, some homebuyers will search the database to see how many sex offenders are in a specific neighborhood or city.

Metes and Bounds System: The metes and bounds system are the boundary lines of a property, with their angles and terminal points. It's a way of describing property by listing the distances and compass directions of the boundaries.

Mile, Rod, Township, Section, and Acre Distances: A mile is 5,280 feet, a rod is 16.5 feet, a township is 36 sections, a section is 640 acres, and an acre is 43,560 square feet. Each of these measurements is utilized for survey maps.

Millage Rate: This is the tax rate used to calculate local property taxes. The millage rate is the amount a homeowner has to pay for every $1,000 of a home's value based on the tax assessment.

Mineral Rights: Mineral rights are the rights given to the owner to mine and exploit all minerals on their land. For example, if there was oil on the land and the property owner had the mineral rights to the land, then they would have a right to drill for that oil. The mineral rights can be sold separately from the property rights.

Misrepresentation: A misrepresentation is when an agent fails to disclose or misstates a particular issue or material defect during a transaction. An agent could intentionally or unintentionally misrepresent part of a real estate transaction. An example of intentional misrepresentation would be if an agent knows a home's foundation is faulty, but fails or refuses to disclose this fact to their client. In both intentional and unintentional misrepresentation, the agent could be held liable in a lawsuit.

Mixed-Use: A kind of development or property that combines residential, commercial, office, entertainment, or other uses.

MLS Listings: The Multiple Listing Service is a private database of properties that are active and sold on the market and used by real estate agents to buy and sell real estate more effectively. There are numerous MLS systems across the United States, and much of the information is synced to public databases such as Zillow and Redfin. However, certain information on the MLS is hidden to protect client privacy, such as client contact information.

Mold: Mold is a harmful fungus that requires moisture to grow and thrive and can be found in properties across the United States. Common areas for mold in a property include the basement and attic. There are different types of mold and different levels of mold, and it is always best to have a home inspector and mold remediation company evaluate the mold and remediate as necessary.

Month-to-Month Tenancy: A month-to-month tenancy is a lease agreement in which the tenant stays and pays the rent one month at a time. This type of tenancy is mostly found in residential leases. Month-to-month tenancies can benefit both the renter and the owner since the renter has more flexibility, and the owner can charge more than a standard lease.

Mortgage Broker: A mortgage broker brings borrowers and lenders together. Mortgage brokers gather different loan options from various lenders and get the necessary financial paperwork from the borrower to get them qualified.

Mortgage Insurance: Insurance that protects the mortgage lender against the losses incurred in the event of a mortgage default. There are different types of mortgage insurances, and typically the higher the loan-to-value ratio on a mortgage, the more likely that a buyer will need mortgage insurance.

Multifamily Home: A multifamily property is a dwelling with multiple units where each such unit has its own bathroom, kitchen, and living area. Multifamily homes range from 2-unit duplexes up to large-scale apartment buildings.

NAHREP: NAHREP is the National Association of Hispanic Real Estate Professionals, an organization dedicated to empowering both Hispanic realtors and Hispanic homeownership in the United States. NAHREP is the largest minority trade group in the real estate industry, with over 30,000 members all over the country.

NAR: The NAR, or National Association of Realtors, is the largest trade organization in the United States, with over 1 million members. The National Association of Realtors includes residential and commercial real estate brokers, agents, appraisers, property managers, and others in the real estate industry.

NAREB: NAREB is the National Association of Real Estate Brokers. It was founded in 1947 by African American people who were discouraged from joining the National Association of Realtors. Today, NAREB is the oldest minority trade organization in the United States.

Negative Amortization: In this scenario, a borrower fails to pay what would cover the principal and the interest on the mortgage. As a result, the unpaid balance will be added to the loan's principal balance.

Negligence: In real estate, negligence is when an agent fails to maintain or execute their professional duties. For example, if a real estate agent discloses information that is supposed to be confidential, or if they fail to inform a seller of other offers, then that would be considered negligent.

Negligent Misrepresentation:
A negligent misrepresentation is when someone makes a false statement without knowing the facts. While the agent might not be lying directly, they are making a statement that they do not know the truth about. For example, if a real estate agent claims that a neighborhood is quiet without any knowledge about whether the area is quiet or not, this can be considered negligent misrepresentation.

Net Lease: In a net lease, a tenant is required to pay a portion or all of the property taxes, insurance, maintenance, and other associated fees. Net leases are most common in commercial real estate, where the owners do not want to handle the logistics of operating their buildings.

Net Listing: A net listing is an agreement that a real estate agent enters into with a seller that would allow the agent to keep the proceeds of a home sale above a specific price. Net listings are generally illegal across the United States.

No-Doc Loans: This refers to loans that don't require the borrowers to provide documentation of their personal income to the lenders, and instead rely on a declaration confirming the buyer can afford the loan. During the subprime mortgage crisis of 2008, no-doc loans were common. Nowadays, no-doc mortgages are not allowed.

NOI: NOI or net operating income is used to analyze how profitable an income-generating real estate investment is. The formula for NOI is taking the gross operating income and subtracting it from the operating expenses. Net operating income is helpful for investors who are buying multifamily or commercial properties.

Non-Conforming Loans: Non-conforming loans are loans (usually mortgage loans) that are above the conforming loan limit. Each lender will have different criteria for non-conforming mortgages, although they will come with higher interest rates because they are riskier for a lender. Non-conforming loans typically require higher down payments and stricter credit criteria. They are also known as jumbo loans.

Non-Conforming Use: Non-conforming use is when a particular property was allowed under the established zoning regulations of the time, but because of changes in the zoning regulations, it would no longer be allowed. Every jurisdiction will have its own rules in regard to properties with non-conforming uses.

Non-Judicial Foreclosure: A non-judicial foreclosure is a foreclosure that does not require the lender to go through the courts to foreclose on a property, and the process is much faster than a judicial foreclosure. Some states require judicial foreclosures which involve court proceedings, and some are non-judicial foreclosure states.

Normal Wear and Tear: This refers to the naturally occurring damage over time that property has when it is rented out to a tenant. Common examples of normal wear and tear would be small stains on a carpet, dirty grout, small scratches on the floor, and small holes or cracks in the drywall. If the property has further damage, such as broken windows or completely damaged flooring, then the landlord would consider taking the tenant's security deposit to fix the damages.

Notary Public: A notary public is someone who is authorized by the federal or state government to administer oaths, as well as to attest to the originality of signatures. Notaries are required for some real estate documents, and at closing, the title agent handling the settlement will also be a notary public.

Notice of Default (NOD): A notification given to a borrower that they are in default on their mortgage. Some lenders will provide a borrower a grace period to make any necessary payments. A notice of default is one of the first steps in a foreclosure proceeding.

Obedience With a Client: Obedience with a client states that an agent must obey any lawful orders provided by the client. However, if the client instructed the agent from showing the property to any minorities, then that would be unlawful, and the agent could lose their license.

One-Hundred-Percent Commission Plan: This is a real estate brokerage business model where the real estate agents under the brokerage keep 100% of their commission. In most standard brokerages, the agent will split their commission with their broker ranging from 50/50 to 75/25 to 90/10 and other arrangements. One-hundred-percent commission brokerages instead charge their agents a low monthly or yearly fee and a small transaction fee for every deal.

Open Listing: An open listing is a non-exclusive agreement that allows an owner to have multiple agents market their property. The owner in this scenario is unrepresented but only has to pay for the broker who brings a buyer to the deal. This type of listing is not very common, and many agents would hesitate to take on an open listing because of the lack of commitment from the seller.

Opinion of Title: An opinion of title is written by a real estate attorney and summarizes if a title is in good legal standing, or what actions need to be taken to place the home in good standing. This is what a title company will do to ensure that the property has marketable title and can be sold.

Opportunity Cost: An economic term that determines the benefits that an individual or entity misses out on when choosing one option over an alternative. Every time someone makes a decision in real estate or elsewhere, they need to think about what they are gaining as well as what they are giving up.

Opportunity Zones: Opportunity zones were created in 2017 by the Tax Cuts and Jobs Act. These zones were created to boost economic development in distressed areas throughout the United States.

Opportunity Zones can provide massive tax incentives to investors who invest eligible funds into those areas.

Option Contract: An option contract provides a buyer with the exclusive right or option to purchase a home at a later date for a given price. The owner cannot sell the property to anyone else during the term of the option, and this type of purchase can be an excellent way for a buyer to lock in a deal while they obtain the funding. If the potential buyer does not buy during the option time frame, then they will lose their option deposit.

Oral Agreement: An agreement without the presence of a written document. While it is possible in some scenarios to create a binding oral contract, in real estate, it is highly advised to have everything in writing.

Origination Fees: An origination fee is a fee paid to a lender, which covers the cost of processing a loan. The origination fee will generally be a fixed amount, usually between .5% and 1% of the total mortgage loan.

Ostensible Agent: Ostensible agency is created when a real estate agent gives a third party reason to believe that they are representing a principal in a transaction even though they are not.

Overimprovement: These are renovations or improvements that are more extensive compared to what the surrounding neighborhood justifies or more extensive than what can be economically warranted. For example, if a seller built a 2,000-square-foot addition onto their property in an area where all the houses were 1,000 square feet, that would be considered overimprovement.

Owner's Title Insurance: This is insurance that protects the owner from any title claims made against the home after closing. Although not required, owner's title insurance can come in handy should there be any legal ramifications.

Parol Evidence Rule: The parol evidence rule stipulates that no evidence may contradict what is written in a contract. Once a contract has been signed, it cannot be changed by additional oral agreements or other understandings unless they are in writing and are part of the contract.

Partition: In real property law, a partition is when two or more landowners cannot agree on the use of land, and an agreement is made to divide the land amongst the owners. This can be a voluntary act, or, if court-ordered, a partition can be mandated to settle a real property dispute.

Passive Income: In real estate, passive income is a result of money earned on rental properties, both residential and commercial. For example, every time a tenant pays rent, the owner is receiving passive income. There are different forms of passive income, and the IRS taxes passive income at a lower rate. It is always recommended to check with your CPA what qualifies as passive income.

Percentage Lease: A percentage lease is where the tenant pays a base rent plus a percent of any revenue they earn while doing business at the property. The base rent is typically lower than what a standard lease would be but offers a potential upside to the landlord and gives the current occupant a reduced rent.

Personal Property: Personal property is moveable property, unlike a fixture. Examples of personal property are furniture, household goods, collectibles, cars, and more. Lenders can take into account personal property assets in addition to a borrower's personal finances when qualifying for a loan.

Pet Deposit: An additional security deposit that covers any damage caused by a pet. In apartments or properties that allow dogs and cats, a pet deposit is standard.

Phishing Scams: In real estate, these are fraudulent email messages that seem to come from legitimate sources such as a lender or title company. Usually, these messages direct the recipient to wire their deposit or closing funds to their account instead of a title company or lender. The best way to prevent this type of scam is to set up two-step authentication with your email and also call the title company to confirm any wiring information.

Physical Life: Physical life is the time period during an asset on a property that can be expected to remain viable and in existence.

PITI: PITI stands for Principal, Interest, Taxes, and Insurance that make up your monthly payment. PITI is your entire monthly mortgage payment and gives a potential buyer and lender a more accurate picture of the total cost of monthly homeownership.

Planned Unit Development (PUD): A PUD is a community of properties that can include both residential and commercial units. Planned unit developments typically have amenities such as playgrounds, tennis courts, and a community center.

The development is operated by a homeowner's association with monthly or quarterly dues to cover the amenities and certain other features such as maintenance and landscaping. A buyer in a PUD will need to review the HOA documents of the PUD before purchasing the home.

Plat: A plat is a scale-drawn map of how property is divided within a piece of land. When you purchase a property, the title company will typically give you a plat along with your closing documents.

PMI: PMI stands for Private Mortgage Insurance and is typically required when a home is purchased with a conventional loan at more than 80% of the property's value. Private mortgage insurance protects the lender if the buyer fails to make payments. The higher the loan amount is compared to the value of the property, the riskier the loan is for the lender.

Pocket Listing: A pocket listing is a practice where a home is for sale, but it is not listed on the MLS. Instead, the agent tries to sell the property through their private network of real estate agents and previous clients who may have an interest in buying. This is utilized when a seller wants to maintain more privacy, and it is a strategy to test the real estate market without going public with the listing.

Points: Also known as mortgage points, points are fees a homebuyer can pay to their lender at closing in exchange for lower interest rates. In most cases, one point gets you .25 off of the current mortgage interest rates, and one point costs 1 percent of the loan amount.

Police Power: Police power provides authority to the state and local government to create and enforce laws for the safety, health, and welfare of the community. Some examples of police power include zoning, building codes, requiring real estate licenses, and even damaging private property without compensation in the event of a fire or other such catastrophes to protect the public interest.

Polybutylene Piping: A form of plastic piping that was used extensively from 1978 until 1995. It is typically grey or white with a dull finish, and over time, it becomes brittle and loses its strength. When a home inspector finds polybutylene piping in a property, they typically recommend replacing all of the piping completely.

Power of Attorney (POA): A power of attorney in real estate is a legal document that allows someone the authority to buy or sell real estate for a person. An example of POA is when a person, maybe an older parent that lives in assisted living, can't make decisions on their own, so they give POA to someone they trust, such as a grown child. Or, if a principal to a transaction is out of the country or lives some distance from the property, they can give power of attorney to someone local that they trust.

Practicing Within Area of Competence: This refers to working in a market or industry that matches one's level of expertise. In real estate, an agent who has typically sold residential property for 20 years would not be in an area of competence if they tried to sell commercial properties.

Pre-Approval: This is a written commitment from the lender for a mortgage after the borrower completes a loan application and has its financial information reviewed. To get a pre-approval, a lender would look at employment, income, credit, and other financial resources. A pre-approval is one step above a pre-qualification, and a pre-approval letter is typically submitted with an offer to show that the buyer can afford the property.

Pre-Qualification: Prequalifying for a loan is usually a soft inquiry into a prospective homebuyer's financial and credit history to see if they will qualify for a home loan. Although pre-qualification is useful, it is not a guarantee of what a buyer will be eligible for. Pre-qualification is a quick process that can be done over the phone or online and is only based on the information you provide to the lender instead of a full mortgage application and review of finances like a pre-approval.

Predatory Lending: Predatory lending involves the unethical practice of coercing or forcing a borrower into unfavorable loan terms. Leading up to the market crash of 2008, there were many instances of predatory lending going on. During that time, the lender benefited in the short term, and the borrower's ability to repay the loan was ignored or downplayed.

Prepayment Penalty: In a mortgage, a prepayment penalty is a fee a homeowner must pay if they choose to pay their loan ahead of schedule. Prepayment penalties allow the lender to collect a fee in lieu of the interest they would earn if the mortgage went full term. Prepayment penalties are not as common in mortgages today. However, you should always confirm with your lender.

Prescriptive Easements: A prescriptive easement is when someone gains an interest in a property by using another party's property for a specific period of time without the other party's consent. This could often happen on large pieces of rural land where the owner does not realize that part of their land is being used. There are strict requirements that vary from state to state regarding prescriptive easements.

Price Fixing: Price fixing is the collective agreement for businesses to set or fix their prices. In real estate, brokers cannot enter into agreements that set their commission or service fees.

Price Per Square Foot: Price per square foot is a way to calculate comparable sales of a property based on the price per square foot of a property. This strategy is more common in condos or apartment buildings than it is with large single-family homes since there are more variables with single-family homes.

Primary Mortgage Market: This is the market where a borrower can get a mortgage from a primary lender such as a bank, mortgage broker, or credit union. In contrast, the secondary mortgage market is where investors can buy and sell mortgages that have already been issued. It is common for a homebuyer's mortgage to be purchased by another lender or mortgage servicing company shortly after closing. Banks sell their mortgages to organizations such as Fannie Mae and other companies to get the mortgage off of their books so that they can lend more.

Prime Rate: The prime rate is the best interest rate available on the market at a given time. Banks will offer the prime rate for mortgages, loans, and credit cards to only their most creditworthy customers.

Principal Broker: A principal broker is a licensed real estate broker who oversees a real estate brokerage and is responsible for the real estate agents in the brokerage. A principal broker also has the required years of experience and additional continuing education to qualify as a broker. Principal brokers are held to higher standards of responsibility than a real estate agent or associate broker.

Principal Residence: This is the main home or property that a homebuyer physically occupies and uses. What a homeowner or occupant declares as their primary residence is important for tax purposes, and you should always consult a CPA. Most mortgages will require that you intend to move into the property that you are getting for a mortgage and make it your principal residence for at least a year.

Principal: A principal is any person involved in a real estate contract, such as a seller or buyer. A real estate agent acts on behalf of a principal in a transaction to put their best interests forward.

Principle of Anticipation: The principle of anticipation is a method used by appraisers, by using the income approach, to determine the value of a property. This approach is based on the future value and benefits of a property because of the monthly and yearly income a property could earn.

Principle of Balance: The principle of balance refers to the relationship between the cost of a renovation and the value that it returns on the property.

Principle of Change: The principal of change is referring to the economic and social forces that affect the value of a property. If a city is experiencing economic growth, the value of the homes will increase, and the opposite is true as well.

Principle of Competition: This principle refers to the idea that excess profits on a real estate deal or business will breed competition that will eventually lower profit margins.

Principle of Conformity: The principle of conformity states that utilizing a real property in a similar manner as the rest of a neighborhood can help protect property value. The principle of conformity is the main reason why homes in specific subdivisions look similar to each other. For example, if there was a 5,000-square-foot modern mansion in a neighborhood of old rancher-styles homes, then that would be worth less than if it was in a similar neighborhood of large modern homes.

Principle of Contribution: The principle of contribution (also referred to as the principle of marginal contribution) is that the worth of a property improvement is what contributes to the market value instead of what it costs to add the improvement. For example, just because a homeowner spent $20,000 on a swimming pool does not mean that their property value has increased with $20,000, since some buyers may not prefer a pool.

Principle of Plottage: Plottage is when multiple pieces of adjoining land are combined to form a single, larger piece of real estate. Typically, this would increase the value, although it is not guaranteed.

Principle of Progression: This is an appraisal term, which means that the value of less expensive homes will increase if more expensive properties come into the neighborhood. It is common for a homebuyer to purchase the cheapest house in a community, with the hope that the surrounding (higher-value) homes will help increase its value.

Principle of Regression: This is an appraisal term, which means the value of a property will decrease if less expensive homes come into the neighborhood. If a buyer purchases an unusually expensive property in an area that does not have expensive homes, then the value of that property will go down.

Principle of Substitution: The principle of substitution is a method used to determine the relative value of a property. This principle states that the maximum value of a property is based on what the price of acquiring a similar property in the same area would be. For example, if all of the updated 3-bedroom townhomes in a neighborhood sell for around 350K, then a buyer will not pay 500K for a comparable townhome. The principle of substitution focuses on the question "what other homes can you buy for the same price?".

Principle of Supply and Demand: The principle of supply and demand is what determines the prices of real estate. When demand is high, and supply is low, the cost of real estate will increase, and vice versa. Things like job growth, new developments, and the economy will have a significant effect on supply and demand.

Pro Forma: A pro forma in real estate is a document with projected investment returns on a specific property or properties. This is often used when an investor or developer needs to raise money from investors for a deal.

Probate: Probate is the legal process of distributing the assets in an estate, including real estate, that takes place after someone dies. Probate properties are often sold at a discount because they need updating, and the executor of the estate does not want to deal with it.

Procuring Cause: A procuring cause in a real estate transaction is the agent who was ultimately responsible for a buyer finding a home, and therefore receives the commission. For example, if a buyer used one agent to show them a house but a different agent to write the contract, then the first agent could make the argument that they were the procuring cause and are entitled to the commission.

Promissory Note: A promissory note is a written agreement which provides a promise to pay back a loan at a specific interest rate within a set time. Promissory notes are included in mortgages and other types of loan agreements.

Property Lien Taxes: Property lien taxes are legal claims against a property due to unpaid property taxes. If a homeowner has not paid their property taxes, the county or city that is owed taxes imposes a property lien that is often public record. After a certain period of nonpayment, the county or city can auction off the tax lien and, eventually, the property.

Property Management: The branch of the real estate business that deals with the management of property. These could include residential rental properties, commercial, or industrial real estate. Landlords will often hire a property manager to collect rent, make any necessary repairs, and find tenants.

Property Survey: Property surveys are used to confirm the boundaries of a property and if there are any restrictions or conditions that apply to the home. Most people will get a survey done as part of buying a home, and many lenders will require one. Surveys are also done when a homeowner is installing a fence or building a structure on a property.

Property Tax Calculations: Property taxes are calculated by multiplying the county and state interest rate by the assessed home value. As an example, in Fairfax County, a $200,000 home with a 1.1 percent tax rate would result in a $2,200 tax bill. The property tax information can be found in the public records of the property.

Property Tax Deduction: This refers to local and state property taxes that are usually deductible from federal income taxes and one of the many benefits of owning real estate. If you purchase real estate, it is always a good idea to meet with a CPA.

Property Taxes: Property taxes are taxes that are levied on real estate property within a local city or county government. These taxes are typically based on the home's value and are almost always included in the mortgage payments.

Proprietary Lease: In a co-op purchase, the buyer is given a property lease to occupy the unit. Since the buyer is technically a shareholder in the corporation and purchasing a share of the corporation instead of acquiring real estate, they are given a proprietary lease.

Protected Classes: According to the Fair Housing Act, seven protected classes are protected from discrimination when buying, selling, or renting a home. These include color, disability, familial status, national origin, religion, race, and sex. Many states have additional protected classes that are protected by the Fair Housing Act as well.

Protection Clause: Also known as an extender clause, this is a contingency found in most listing contracts that protect a broker's right to a commission in most situations, even if the property sells after the listing period ends. The clause is put in there to prevent a seller from dragging their feet and waiting until the listing expires to sell the property. It usually only applies if the end buyer was introduced to the property by the listing broker and then later buys it within a short time frame after the expiration of the listing.

Public Utility Easement: This is a common type of easement that grants specific rights to a utility company to access a property for utility purposes. For example, if a utility company needs to make repairs to underground pipes or access overhead electrical lines, they would have access through a public utility easement.

Puffing: Puffing is the exaggeration of certain traits or facts about a property. For example, if an agent shows a property and says, "This is the nicest kitchen I've ever seen," then they could be exaggerating to make the home seem nicer. Puffing is not typically illegal unless the statements are outright fraudulent.

Punch List: A punch list is a list of the final items on a property before it is ready to be listed or sold. Usually, a punch list would include smaller items such as fixing the dishwasher, replacing nonfunctioning lights, professionally cleaning the property, replacing a broken window, and other items to get a house ready to be sold.

Purchase Money Mortgage: This is a mortgage in which the seller of a home provides the financing to the buyer. If a buyer is unable to qualify for a home loan, the seller can opt to lend the money to the buyer through seller financing in a purchase money mortgage.

Qualified Buyer: A qualified buyer is a prospective buyer that has been preapproved and has enough money for a down payment and closing costs.

Quitclaim Deed: A quitclaim deed is a document stating that a person is giving up their interest in a property. In other words, it "quits" an interest in the piece of real estate. Quitclaim deeds are most often used among family members or divorcing couples.

R-Value: R-Value is a measure of how well insulation, windows, or other material can resist heat. The higher the R-Value, the better the insulation it has. Most homes, especially those built before 1980, would not meet the insulation and R-Value standards of present-day construction.

Radon Test: A radon test is a standard test done during a real estate transaction to find out if there is any radon in the property. Radon is a tasteless, odorless, and colorless radioactive element that is the second leading cause of lung cancer deaths in the US. The test involves an inspector or homeowner placing a radon testing cannister in the basement for a few days and then sending those results to a lab. While small amounts of radon can be found in homes, if the radon level is above 4.0 pCi/l, then the EPA recommends remediation.

Radon: Radon is a tasteless, odorless, and colorless radioactive element that is the second leading cause of lung cancer deaths in the US. When a property is bought or sold on the market, a radon test is commonly done along with a home inspection. If radon is found in the property, it is typically easy to mitigate by installing a radon system in the basement. Another way to limit the exposure to radon is for homes to be well-ventilated both inside and around the house.

Ratification: Ratification occurs when a contract has been fully signed by both parties and delivered to both the buyer and seller. When a buyer and seller are in the negotiation stage, giving counteroffers, the property is not yet ratified, and another offer with better terms could be presented, which the seller could take.

Ready, Willing, and Able: This is a phrase often mentioned in listing agreements to state the kind of buyer a real estate broker is looking to find. Both brokers and sellers want to find potential buyers who fit this statement because it reveals they're dealing with someone qualified and prepared to make an offer. If a seller rejects an offer from a ready, willing, and able buyer who is prepared to meet the seller's terms, the listing agent could still be entitled to a commission.

Real Estate Agent: A real estate agent is someone who is licensed to sell real estate and works under a real estate broker. The real estate agent requirements will vary from state to state, although the requirements to become licensed include being at least 18 years of age, a US citizen, having complete pre-licensing education requirements, and passing the real estate test.

Real Estate Broker: A real estate broker can work independently or hire agents for real estate transactions. To become a broker, one must work as a real estate agent full time for several years and also take additional continuing education courses and pass a state licensing broker exam.

Real Estate Commission: A commission is the percentage of a real estate transaction that is paid to the agent(s) involved in the sale of a home. Typically, the commission is between 5 and 6% total of the sale price. That means that the buyer's agent in a transaction would earn 2.5%-3% of the final sales price, and the listing agent would earn the other half of the commission upon a successful closing. However, real estate commission is negotiable and can be any amount that the listing agent and seller decide upon in writing.

Real Estate Cycles: A series of periodic events reflected in economic, demographic, and emotional factors, which influence supply and demand for real estate and home values. The real estate market has historically been cyclical and goes through a recovery phase, expansion phase, hyper supply phase, and then a recession phase. The four cycles do not happen in equal time periods and will also vary depending on the location and type of property.

Real Estate Salesperson: Also known as a real estate agent, a real estate salesperson must be licensed in the state they are working in, and they must hang their real estate license under a broker to represent clients in real estate transactions.

Realtor Code of Ethics: The realtor code of ethics was created by the National Association of Realtors and sets the standard for business practices of realtors. When a real estate agent wants to become a realtor, they must pay NAR a membership fee and adhere to the Realtor Code of Ethics.

Realtor: A realtor is a real estate agent who is also a member of the National Association of Realtors. To become a realtor, an agent needs to pay a fee to the National Association of Realtors and adhere to their code of ethics.

Reasonable Care: Reasonable care is a required fiduciary duty by a real estate agent to ensure that the client is protected from foreseeable harm. A real estate agent is deemed to have more skill and expertise compared to an average person in a real estate transaction and is obligated to treat their client with professionalism.

Rebate: A rebate is when a real estate agent gives back a portion of their commission to a buyer. This is how discount real estate companies do their real estate transactions. Rebates can range anywhere from a few hundred dollars to upwards of half or more of a commission that an agent would earn.

Recorder of Deeds: A government office responsible for maintaining documents and public records, particularly records associated with real estate ownership.

Recovery Fund: Recovery funds are designed to help reimburse anyone who was a victim of monetary damages caused by a real estate agent or broker during a real estate transaction that violates state real estate law. Examples of eligible grievances include misappropriated funds, repair costs due to misrepresentation, and any other type of deceit by an agent during a transaction.

Redlining: A discriminatory practice, typically involving lenders who refuse to extend credit or lend money to borrowers in specific areas of town. In other words, redlining is the practice of denying entire communities, neighborhoods, or subdivisions access to mortgages and loans.

Referral Fee: A referral fee is provided to a real estate agent when they refer a client to another agent, and they purchase or sell a property. If an agent is too busy to take on leads or the leads are in a different city, the agent might refer the lead to another real estate agent who would pay them a referral fee after closing. Typical referral fees are around 20% of the net commission.

Refinancing: Refinancing is when a homeowner takes out a new mortgage to replace their original mortgage. This strategy is popular since it can lower a homeowner's monthly payment, give them access to cash for home renovations, get rid of mortgage insurance premiums, and overall give a homeowner more favorable terms. There are different types of refinancing available, and if interest rates have dropped and the buyer has earned equity in their property, then it could make sense to refinance the loan.

Regulation Z: Regulation Z is a part of the Truth in Lending Act of 1968, and it is designed to protect borrowers and consumers from unscrupulous practices from the lending industry. It requires credit card companies, mortgage issuers, and other lenders to provide written disclosure of basic credit terms like interest rate, fees, and additional pertinent financial information on a loan.

Reissue Rate: A reissue rate is a homebuyer discount on the cost of their owner's title insurance policy. If the previous owner purchased the property and got owner's title insurance within the last 10 years, then the reissue rate is typically available to the new buyer. A title company should automatically look into seeing if the reissue rate is available, although it is always a good idea to remind them to look into it.

REIT: A REIT is a Real Estate Investment Trust. These are entities that own income properties and are traded on major stock exchanges. Most REITs specialize in a specific type of real estate, such as multifamily apartments, hotels, office buildings, self-storage, or others. Investors can purchase shares of REITs similarly to the way they would buy any publicly traded stock.

Remainderman: This term refers to a person who inherits or will inherit property upon the death of the former owner. The person to whom the property will be transferred to is the remainderman. The current owner will have to create a life estate to grant ownership to a remainderman.

Rent Back: A rent back is when a seller of the home rents from the new buyer after closing, usually for 30-60 days to give them some extra flexibility to move to their next property. Rent back agreements are common, and the seller will put a security deposit into escrow in case there is any damage during their time after closing. Sometimes a buyer will give a seller a free rent back, and sometimes the seller will pay a per-diem charge of the buyer's financing costs pro-rated over the time they stay there.

Rent Control: Rent control puts a limit on how much a landlord can charge tenants and is only allowed in a few large cities in the US that have high rents, such as San Francisco, New York City, DC, and a few others. However, when a tenant moves out of a rent-controlled property, the landlord is usually allowed to increase the rent to the market rate. Rent control is a controversial law, and each area will have particular regulations on how their rent control program works.

REO: REO stands for real estate owned, and it is property taken back by a lender when a home isn't sold at a foreclosure auction. Even though the lender will try to sell the properties at a discount at auctions, they don't always sell, and so the lender will have to list the property with an REO agent. These properties are usually sold "as is" and can be bought below market value since they need work.

Replacement Value: Replacement value or replacement cost is determined by how much it would cost to replace and rebuild a property. For example, replacement value insurance would not factor in the market value of a particular property, just the cost to rebuild it. Replacement cost is typically part of a homeowner's insurance policy.

Requirements for a Listing Agreement: A valid listing agreement should contain a starting and ending date for listing the property, the list price, the broker's compensation, the services to be provided for listing the property, and the agreement must be in writing.

Requirements for Validity in a Contract: A contract must have specific criteria to be valid, including capable parties, lawful in nature, consideration, and offer and acceptance. If a contract is missing any of these pieces, it could be deemed void.

Rescind: To rescind a contract means to withdraw or cancel the offer. For example, if a buyer decided to rescind their offer, they would have to send a withdrawal notice before the seller accepts their offer.

Reserves: Reserves are the liquid funds available to pay for future renovations and expenses at a condo building or HOA community. Reserves are funded by condo and HOA dues. When a buyer purchases a property from a condo or HOA, they will receive a disclosures packet that shows how much money the association has in reserves.

Restrictive Covenant: A type of agreement that needs the buyer to either abstain from or take a specific action. It is a binding legal obligation written into the deed of a real estate property by the seller. Restrictive covenants can be either complex or simple, and penalties can be imposed against the buyers who fail to adhere to them. Some of these covenants could include exterior paint colors, the number of tenants who can live in a property, commercial activity at a property, and more. A buyer might find a restrictive covenant in an HOA community or a historic district.

Retaliatory Eviction: This type of eviction is not based on any actual breach of the lease but is instead based on the landlord retaliating against a tenant enforcing their legal rights. Some of these rights could include a tenant filing a complaint with a building inspector about illegal living conditions and organizing a tenant union. Retaliatory evictions are illegal in just about every state, and some landlords would try to increase the rent, harass the tenant, cut off amenities and services, or file to evict the tenant.

Reverse Mortgage: A reverse mortgage is a loan that allows specific homeowners to borrow money against the equity in their home. The borrower does not make monthly payments, and instead, the lender makes monthly payments to the borrower. To be eligible for a reverse mortgage, the borrower must be at least 62 years old and either own their home outright or have a significant amount of equity in their home.

Reversion: Reversion is when the ownership of a trust or property is reverted, or given back to the original trustee after a temporary ownership period. For example, if an owner gave a property to Jacob "for life," then upon Jacob's death, the property reverts back to the original owner or their heirs.

Revocation: Revocation is a withdrawal of an offer or contract from either party. For example, when a buyer withdraws an offer on a home, it is a revocation.

Rezoning: Rezoning is the process of changing the primary purpose of a property or piece of land. An owner or developer would want to rezone a property for various reasons, including developing condos, changing from commercial to residential, and a myriad of other reasons. The rezoning process varies from city to city and usually involves an application, public meetings with the zoning or planning commission, and legislative approval.

Right of First Refusal: The right of first refusal allows a specific party (or tenant) the right to purchase a property if it is ever offered for sale. Before a seller puts a property up for sale on the market, they have to notify the original interested buyer who can decide if they want to purchase it.

Right of Redemption: A buyer's right of redemption allows a borrower to repurchase their home after foreclosure or tax sale from the individual who bought the house at auction. Every state will have different time periods and procedures for the right of redemption.

Right of Survivorship: The right of survivorship is real estate attribute associated with joint ownership, where, should one of the owners die, the other owner automatically takes their share of the home. When a husband and wife own a home, and one of them passes away, if a right of survivorship is in place, the surviving spouse assumes full ownership.

Riparian Rights: Riparian rights are the rights that owners have with land adjacent to a waterway, such as a river or a stream. The rights include the reasonable use of the waterways, including swimming, boating, fishing, and irrigation. These rights are also held in common with other riparian owners.

Roof Type: Refers to the material or covering on the roof of a building, house, or condo. The type of roof is mentioned on most real estate listings. Roofs can vary from the standard asphalt shingles to metal roofing, synthetic roofing, slate roofing, wood shingles, and more.

Sales Comparison Approach: Refers to a process used to determine the present market value of a property based on the recent sales of comparable properties in that area. When a real estate agent analyzes comps for a client, they are using a sales comparison approach.

Scarcity: In economics, scarcity is the limited quantity or availability of a particular good, service, or activity. In regard to real estate, homes, land, and other real property that have scarcity will drive up the demand and the price.

Second Mortgage: This is a lien on a property whose position is second to that of the original mortgage. Second mortgages are typically home equity lines of credit or a simple one-time loan that is secured against the property. To qualify for a second mortgage, the property would need to have a good amount of equity to secure the second mortgage. Since these loans are riskier, they come with higher interest rates.

Secondary Mortgage Market: The secondary mortgage market is when a homebuyer's mortgage loan gets sold to an investor such as Fannie Mae, Freddie Mac, and others. When a buyer obtains a mortgage for the purchase of their property, that is known as the primary market. The way the lender recoups their funds is that they sell the loan, along with other similar loans, as a mortgage-backed security to large investment firms and insurance companies. This gives the original lender the funds to make additional mortgage loans. It is common for a buyer's mortgage to be sold on the secondary mortgage market.

Section 8: This is a program that allows landlords to rent their property at market value to qualified low-income tenants. The tenants can pay through a rental voucher given to them by the US Department of Housing and Urban Development (HUD). To get approved for Section 8, the residents have to submit an application and qualify. The landlord's property also has to meet Section 8 criteria, including being a safe and livable property. This program is popular with landlords because the rental income is often guaranteed every month through the government.

Self-Dealing: Self-dealing refers to the practice of a real estate agent acting in their own best interests in a transaction instead of the best interests of their client. This is illegal and a conflict of interest in real estate deals. An example of self-dealing could be if an agent represents both parties in a transaction so that they can get both sides of the commission but does not disclose this information.

Seller Carryback Loans: This is referred to as seller carryback financing, and it means that a seller acts as the bank and carries a second mortgage for the buyer. If a buyer can't fully qualify for financing, the seller can offer a seller carryback loan to make up for the difference if the conventional lender won't finance the full amount. The interest rate on a seller carryback loan is typically higher than a traditional loan because there is more risk. However, if the buyer has a good credit history, it can be a win-win scenario.

Septic System: These are underground wastewater treatment systems that are common in rural areas that don't have public sewer systems. A septic system consists of a septic tank and a drain field, and each state has different disclosure laws regarding septic systems. It is essential for a buyer always to get a septic inspection done on a home with septic since an improperly maintained system can be expensive to repair.

Setback: Setbacks are the minimum distance or clearance that has to be maintained from a property line, boundary, transportation route, structure, or other geographic feature. These are part of the building codes, and a setback would prevent an owner from building an additional structure next to a neighbor's property.

Severance Damages: Severance damages is compensation paid to a land or property owner to cover losses incurred after the condemnation of part of the owner's land from the local government. For example, if the government takes some land to make room for a new highway, the owner should be compensated for the value of the part of the property that was taken, as well as the loss of the overall property value caused by the loss.

Sheriff's Deed: A sheriff's deed is a deed that provides ownership to a buyer at a Sheriff's sale. Sheriff's sales are foreclosure auctions that are typically held at the county's courthouse steps. However, there is a redemption period for most sheriff's sales that allow the original owner to make sufficient payments to reclaim their property.

Sherman Act of 1890: Sherman Act of 1890 is an antitrust law that prohibits businesses from manipulating markets through monopolization, price-fixing, or restricting trade. For example, in real estate, if brokers and agents colluded to set their commission percentage at a specific rate, this would be a violation of the Sherman Antitrust Act.

Short Sale: A short sale is a home or other property that is sold for less than what is owed by the owner. A short sale allows both the owner of the house and the bank to avoid going through the lengthy foreclosure process. Not all lenders will accept short sales, and the owner will have to prove distress that they can no longer make their payments. With short sales, it can take up to 6 months for a bank to approve the transaction, and if a buyer is patient, they can sometimes get a great deal.

Single Agent: The most common type of real estate agency, a single agent must represent either the buyer or the seller in a real estate transaction. They cannot represent both sides. A dual agency would be where one agent represents both parties in a real estate transaction, and dual agency is illegal in some states and requires additional paperwork in other states.

Special Agent: A real estate broker is an example of a special agent and is limited to only one specific activity in a real estate transaction. For example, a listing agent is allowed to market and sell a property for the principal. This is in contrast to a general agent or universal agent, who have additional responsibilities on behalf of a principal.

Special Assessment: This is a charge to homeowners in a condo or HOA community to pay for upgrades outside of the current budget. Special assessment fees could go towards a new roof, a new lobby area, new windows, or other costs associated with a building or community. Special assessments must be disclosed in the condo or HOA documents. Another type of special assessment is when a local city charges homeowners for public utility upgrades, road maintenance, and other public services.

Special Warranty Deed: In a special warranty deed, the seller (grantor) does not guarantee that there are any defects in a warranty outside of their period of ownership. For example, if a seller possessed the home for 5 years, a special warranty deed states that they are not liable for any defects found before they owned the home. These types of deeds are common with commercial property. For residential property, a general warranty deed is standard, which covers the entire history of the property.

Specific Lien: A specific lien, unlike a general lien, is put only on a particular piece of property when a debt is owed. For example, a mortgage is a specific lien and does not apply to other assets that an owner may have.

Specific Performance: When a real estate contract is breached, the harmed party may choose specific performance instead of monetary damages, which requires that a contract be fulfilled. In real estate, if the seller breaches the contract and refuses to sell, the buyer can ask the judge for the seller to fulfill the contract and sell the property instead of collecting monetary damages.

Spot Zoning: Spot zoning is when a small piece of land or property is allowed a different type of zoning than what it was originally intended for. Typically, a court or planning commission would have to approve any spot zoning since the zoning may be at odds with the master plan of the city and the surrounding area. An example of spot zoning could be if an owner wanted to develop a commercial property in a strictly residential area.

Statute of Frauds: The Statute of Frauds requires that real estate contracts be completed in writing to be enforceable. Verbal agreements are not enough to prove a real estate contract.

Statute of Limitations: The Statute of Limitations refers to the maximum amount of time any party can take legal action against another party. For example, if a seller didn't disclose material defects in a property, a buyer would only have a set period of time to make a claim against them. The Statute of Limitation laws vary from state to state.

Steering: In real estate, steering is the illegal practice of when a real estate agent guides or "steers" clients towards or away from a particular neighborhood based on their race.

Stigmatized Properties: This is a property that is ignored by buyers for reasons not involving the conditions of the home. Common examples of stigmatized properties include a recent homicide in the house, the neighbors or neighborhood, a belief that the home is haunted, or other misfortunes. Since a stigmatized property does not affect the structure or condition of the house, a seller or real estate agent is typically not required to disclose a stigmatized home. However, each state will have different disclosure laws.

Sub-Agent: A sub-agent is an agent who provides real estate services to a buyer but is actually representing the seller in a transaction. This method of real estate was popular before the 1990s and is no longer common because of the inherent conflict of interest.

Subject To: "Subject to" occurs when a seller's existing financing is taken over by an investor. The investor takes the title to the property, but the loan still stays in the name of the seller. A seller would sell "subject to" if they were highly motivated and did not want to deal with the property anymore. An investor would be interested in "subject to" because they could pick up a good real estate deal, and they wouldn't have to qualify through a bank. There is some risk with this type of scenario since a bank could call in the due on sale clause upon a transfer of a property. The new investor could also miss a payment, which would damage the seller's credit.

Subletting: This is when a tenant rents out the property to another individual. Subletting would be done if the current renter suddenly needed to move for a new job or another reason, and they don't want to break their lease. Every lease agreement will have a different policy in regard to allowing subletting, and most contracts will require the landlord's approval. In a subletting scenario, the original tenant would still have their name on the lease and would be responsible for making payments and keeping the property in the current condition.

Subordination Clause: A subordination clause is a clause in a mortgage which states that the current claim on any debts will take priority over any other claims formed in other agreements made in the future. That means that the original mortgage will be in the first position if the borrower defaults. If a buyer were to get a home equity line of credit or a second mortgage, then that lien would be in the second position after the first mortgage.

Subprime Lending Crisis: The subprime lending crisis occurred around 2005 up until the Great Recession in 2009, when lenders began approving borrowers for mortgages who had high credit risk. Lenders sold these loans as mortgage-backed securities to investment banks, which would then give the lenders more money to lend out for mortgages. Eventually, real estate prices fell, and millions of borrowers were not able to afford their homes any longer, leading to foreclosures nationwide.

Subprime Loan: A subprime loan is a type of loan that is offered to borrowers who do not qualify for a traditional prime rate loan. Subprime loans have higher interest rates than a traditional loan because the borrowers typically have lower credit scores and other factors that a lender would determine they'd be more likely to default on a loan.

Suit for Specific Performance: In a real estate contract, if one party breaches the terms of the agreement, the other party may not want money but instead want the performance of the contract. A court can decide to enforce the contract, and an example could be if a seller decides they no longer wish to sell the property after going under contract with a buyer.

Suit to Quiet Title: A suit to quiet title is a legal claim which sets to establish ownership of a property and serves as a notice against anyone else who might have an interest in the property. When there is a disagreement about ownership, someone would file this suit to settle the title disagreement and remove or "quiet" any other claims to the property.

Supply and Demand: Supply and demand is a well-known economic pricing model that determines the price of real estate in a given area. If the demand for property is high, but there are not many properties, then the prices go up, and it is known as a seller's market. For example, when Amazon announced its new headquarters location, the properties in the neighboring community skyrocketed. When there is too much supply and not enough demand, then it is a buyer's market, and prices go down. In New York City, for example, there was an overflow of new condo developments, which caused prices to go down.

Sweat Equity: Sweat equity occurs when a homeowner improves the value of their property through their own efforts. For example, doing landscaping projects, replacing or refinishing hardwood floors, and replacing windows adds sweat equity to a property.

Syndication: This is a form of real estate investing where a group of real estate investors pool their money together to invest jointly in a project which is led by a sponsor. Similar to crowdfunding, syndication provides an opportunity for investors to buy real estate they may not be able to afford on their own. The sponsor is typically responsible for finding an excellent deal opportunity, raising the money, managing the project, and returning the yield at the end of the deal.

Tax Sale: This is the public sale of a property at auction after a period of nonpayment of property taxes. There are two types of tax sales, including a tax lien sale and a tax deed sale. At a tax lien sale, the winning bidder would have the legal right to collect on the tax lien and interest and could eventually take over the property if the owner was unable to pay. At a tax deed sale, the entire property, including the unpaid taxes, would be sold to the winning bidder. However, each state will have its own redemption period for the owner to get caught up on the taxes and reclaim the property after the auction occurs.

Tenancy at Sufferance: An agreement in which a real estate property renter is legally allowed to live on a property after the expiration of a lease term but before the landlord demands that the tenant vacate the property. A tenant would continue to live in the property and pay rent even after the lease agreement expires.

Tenancy at Will: This is an agreement where a tenant stays at a property without a signed contract or lease. A tenancy at will can be terminated at any time by either the owner or the tenant. Tenancy at will is the same as estate at will, and this arrangement can give an owner and tenant more flexibility. This is commonly just a verbal agreement, which requires the most trust of any type of lease agreement.

Tenancy by the Entirety: This is a method of owning a property that is popular with married couples and available in many states. Each spouse holds an undivided and equal interest in the property, together with the right of survivorship, which gives the surviving spouse the legal right to acquire the deceased spouse's share in the property.

Tenancy for Years: This refers to a lease for a specific period of time. In this arrangement, no notice to vacate is required for termination since the renter is aware of the termination date from the beginning of the lease.

Tenancy in Common: This type of ownership is when two or more people own a property. Each person can have a different percentage of the property, and they are allowed to transfer their share of the property to anyone upon their death or otherwise. This type of ownership is much different than a joint tenancy, where the ownership of the decedent's property automatically goes to the remaining partner.

Tenancy in Severalty: This refers to the sole and absolute ownership of a property by a legal entity or person, without joint tenants, cotenants, or partners. This is the most complete form of ownership.

Term Loan: A term loan is a loan with regular payments, paid over a fixed period of time. For example, a 30-year mortgage with a fixed interest rate is a term loan.

Termination of Agency: There are several different ways to terminate an agency agreement between a real estate agent and a client. The first is the successful completion of the deal, or in other words, the closing. Another way to terminate agency is through a mutual agreement where both parties can agree to terminate the agency, regardless of the reason. A third way to terminate agency is through expiration, if the agreement to sell or buy a property has expired, then that would terminate the agency. A fourth way to terminate agency would be through events such as death, bankruptcy, or destruction of the property. Lastly, an agency can be terminated through the force of law by one of the parties.

Tertiary Market: Tertiary markets are smaller metropolitan areas that are not large enough to be a primary or secondary market. These markets are not as developed; however, there is a potential for high returns since they are more affordable and sometimes more stable.

Testator: A testator is someone who writes a last will and testament. When an individual meets with an attorney to complete their will, the individual becomes the testator.

Third-Party Origination: This term refers to the situation where a lender utilizes another party to partially or wholly originate, underwrite, process, fund, package, or close the mortgages. Many lenders outsource their mortgage origination to a third party, although the process has come under some scrutiny because of the lack of oversight.

Three Characteristics of Land: Three characteristics of land are immobility, indestructibility, and uniqueness. Immobility, which means the land cannot be moved, and the location of the land will profoundly impact its value. Indestructibility means that land cannot be destroyed. The property or improvements on the land can be destroyed, but the land will still be there. Uniqueness means that every piece of land is different in terms of its shape, size, and other factors.

TILA: TILA is an acronym for the Truth In Lending Act of 1968, which was passed as a means to protect consumers from a lack of disclosure on behalf of creditors and lenders. The act has been amended many times and applies to mortgages as well as other types of loans and credit. TILA gives borrowers clear information from lenders as to the costs associated with their mortgage or loan and has additional provisions to restrict lenders from deceptive practices.

Time Is of the Essence: A phrase often used in real estate contracts, which means performance by one party within the time period mentioned in the contract is necessary to seek performance by the other party. If the party does not act within the required time frame, then that could be a breach of the contract. For example, a buyer is expected to complete their home inspection and financing contingency requirements within the allotted time specified in the contract.

Timeshare: A timeshare is a vacation property where a buyer has partial ownership and shares the cost of the property with others. The ownership is given in the form of a shared deed where each owner is usually given priority to use the property during a specific week or weeks throughout the year.

Title Search: A title search is an examination of the public records of a property, including the history of the deed, county records, liens, and any other notices. Before closing on a property, a title company will do a title search to ensure the property's legal ownership and that there is a clean title for the new buyer.

Title Theory: When a home is in a title theory state, the title is held by the mortgage company until the loan is paid in full. In other words, when someone buys a home, the lender technically holds the title until the property is paid off. Some states are title theory states, and some states are lien theory states where a borrower holds the deed to the property.

Townhouse: Also known as a row house, a townhouse is typically a two- or three-level dwelling that shares at least one wall with another unit. For example, San Francisco homes that hug each other near the street are commonly known as townhouses. Newer townhouse communities can come with amenities such as a swimming pool or community center and also have an HOA fee associated with them.

Transfer Tax: Transfer tax is a tax levied on the exchange of title from one party to the new owner. Transfer taxes can vary by state or city and are a one-time fee that a seller and buyer would pay at closing depending on the location.

Transferability: Transferability is one of the four characteristics of property value. For a piece of real estate to have value, the owner must be able to convey it to another owner upon a sale.

TRID: TRID is part of the Truth in Lending Act, which became law as part of the Dodd-Frank Consumer Protection Act and became effective in 2015. It is also known as the "know before you owe" mortgage disclosure rule and was put in place to make it easier for buyers to understand the total costs involved with their loan. One of the main changes is that this law made it a requirement for borrowers to receive their closing information at least 3 business days before settlement so that they have time to review the numbers.

Trust Account: A trust account, also known as an escrow account, is an account managed by a third party during a transaction. For example, a trust account is used when a buyer places any earnest money funds required before closing in to the account. The majority of the time, a title company is responsible for overseeing the trust or escrow account; however, if the account is with the real estate brokerage, then it is the principal broker's responsibility.

UETA: UETA stands for the Uniform Electronic Transactions Act, a federal law whose purpose is to align all states with similar practices for approving the validity of digital signatures. This act made electronic signatures legally enforceable on most real estate contracts.

Unenforceable Contract: An unenforceable contract is a contract that can be voided. There are numerous reasons why a contract could be unenforceable before a court of law, including having an oral contract instead of a written agreement, a lack of consideration or earnest money deposit, lack of mental capacity from one of the principals in the transaction, and many other scenarios.

Uniform Residential Landlord and Tenant Act: Known by its acronym URLTA, this act was created in 1972 to standardize the rights and responsibilities for both tenants and landlords. There are six articles in the URLTA, covering obligations for the tenant and landlord, as well as remedies for both parties.

Unilateral Agreement: A unilateral agreement involves only one party making a promise to perform. This is in contrast to a bilateral agreement, where both parties agree to perform. An example in real estate would be an open listing where a seller agrees to pay a commission to any broker who brings a ready, willing, and able buyer.

Uniqueness: Uniqueness is one of the three physical characteristics of land and states that land is not uniform; it differs in size, shape, and location. An example of uniqueness is that two identical houses in the same development are still in different locations and could have different values as a result.

Universal Agent: A universal agent has a power of attorney and can act fully on behalf of a client or principal to buy or sell property. Each principal to a transaction can only have one universal agent, and this type of arrangement is not common.

Urban Renewal: This is a process where dilapidated parts of an urban area are replaced or renovated in accordance with a master plan for a city. This could include new parks, new housing, renovation of old buildings, new walkways, and more.

Usury Lending Laws: Usury lending laws regulate how much interest a lender can charge borrowers. Lending laws are designed to protect consumers from unfavorably high interest rates.

VA Loan: A VA (Veterans Affairs) loan is a mortgage that is guaranteed by the United States Department of Veterans Affairs. The intention of these loans is to supply home financing to eligible veterans and to help veterans purchase properties with no down payment. This is a common type of financing for veterans.

Valid Contract: A valid real estate contract requires several key functions. There must be an agreement in writing signed by all principals to the transaction, the parties must be competent, there must be consideration (usually an earnest money deposit), and the contract must be for a legal purpose, such as buying a home, and entered into freely without duress or a threat.

Variance: In real estate, a variance is a written request for landowners to deviate from current zoning laws in regard to their property. If the county or city grants the variance, it allows the zoning requirements to be circumvented for that property only. Some examples of a variance are building a structure on vacant property, altering a building so that the building can be used under a new zoning classification, or adding to the exterior of a building through an addition.

Voidable Contract: A voidable contract is a signed contract between two parties, which may be rendered unenforceable for different types of legal reasons. Reasons may include fraud or misrepresentation, undue influence, as well as contingencies in a contract. These contingencies include a home inspection, financing contingency, and appraisal contingency, which could render the contract void if the contingencies do not get met.

Voluntary Liens: Voluntary liens are a claim that one person has over the owner of a property as security for the payment of a debt, and these types of liens are consensual. An example of a voluntary lien would be a mortgage loan for the purchase of real estate or a loan to purchase a vehicle.

What Does a Title Attorney Do? Title attorneys provide a variety of services to ensure that real estate transactions and title transfers are handled correctly. Title attorneys will examine the title to a property, review purchase and sale agreements, coordinate closings, record and disburse funds, and more. Every title company is required to have an attorney on its staff.

Who Pays the Realtor Commission? In standard sales, the home seller is responsible for paying the commission for both the buyer and the seller.

Winterizing: This is the process of preparing a vacant house for cold weather. It includes emptying the pipes throughout the house so that they don't freeze and adding anti-freeze if necessary. Foreclosure properties are often winterized by the bank to prevent any further loss in value.

Wraparound Mortgage: Wraparound loans or wraparound mortgages are junior mortgages that include the current loan on the property, plus an additional loan that covers the price of the property. The buyer's new mortgage "wraps around" the existing home loan. These mortgages are often used in seller financing scenarios.

Zoning Laws: Zoning laws define how a specific area can be utilized within a city, county, or state. These zoning laws can also stipulate other factors, such as building height and lot size. Typical zones can include residential, commercial, administrative, and industrial.

NEXT STEPS

You have reached the end of this guide. For further training materials, including helpful videos, free resources, online education programs, and much more, please visit www.therealestatetrainingteam.com. If you enjoyed this guide, please also leave a helpful review.